Watching for the Morning

Global Chaos and Cosmic Hope

Philip Blair

The Lutterworth Press

Cambridge

First Published in 1999 by:
The Lutterworth Press
P.O. Box 60
Cambridge
CB1 2NT
England

e-mail: **publishing@lutterworth.com**
website: **http://www.lutterworth.com**

ISBN 0 7188 3000 8

British Library Cataloguing in Publication Data:
A catalogue record is available from the British Library.

© Philip Blair, 1999

Cover Design by Catherine Hutton

Quotations
Bible quotations are taken from the Revised Standard Version (RSV)
unless otherwise indicated. Other versions referred to are
the Revised Version (RV) and the Authorised or King James Version (AV)

The quotation in Chapter VII from *The Last Battle* by C.S. Lewis is
reproduced with the permission of HarperCollins Publishers.

Printed in England by
Redwood Books, Trowbridge

Contents

'Watchman, what of the night?' The watchman says:

'Morning comes, and also the night.'

Isaiah 21:11,12

Foreword

Long ago a prisoner on an island in the Mediterranean was shown 'things which must shortly come to pass'. The last strange book of the Christian Bible is the record of that vision. Now on another island in those same warm seas and beneath the same clear skies another writer has taken up that theme of what is to come. The Revelation of St. John the Divine was written on the island of Patmos. Philip Blair wrote this book in Cyprus. Perhaps you don't have to live on a Mediterranean island to contemplate 'the last things' but it certainly helps, if only because you can step outside and see the stars.

Most Christians, fearful of being thought indifferent to this world's needs or of being regarded as crackpots, shy away from serious reflection on what the future holds. This reluctance to look forward is a threefold tragedy. First, never to look beyond the here and now goes against the grain of our human nature. We are made for more than even the best this life affords. After we have thanked God for present blessings in abundance it is not ingratitude to long for what we know we still lack, even though we cannot name it. Secondly, to focus exclusively on what is going on now is to defy the fundamental orientation of Christian faith. That faith is through and through utopian. The future hope is the keystone to the great edifice of Christian theology and without it what we claim to believe collapses into incoherence. Thirdly – and rightly Philip Blair makes much of this – if we disregard what we are one day promised we deny ourselves the resources to meet this day's demands. Jesus taught his disciples to recognise the menacing realities of the present but at the same time to *see through them* to what is to come. We must face the worst now and accept all that it requires of us. But this world's pain will surely break our hearts unless we bear it in the joyful hope of the best that is yet to be.

The accusation that the heavenly-minded fail to take this world seriously cannot be laid against the author of this book. Beginning with the Middle East, a region he knows intimately and has long loved and served, Philip Blair offers a wide-ranging panorama of the plight of our planet at the turn of the millennium. Dr. Blair has an acute sense of the direction in which we are drifting. He traces the currents that propel contemporary culture and he warns us that some of these are sweeping us towards catastrophe. But he is bold enough to claim that all is not out of control. He holds that the Bible both offers a map of the tides of history and also testifies to one who, having allowed himself to be engulfed by those tides, yet proved their master. Not everyone will share the author's approach to the Bible – although it has to be added that those sufficiently old-fashioned to apply the letter of the Bible to the troubles of the world find themselves, somewhat to their surprise, joined these days by the avant-garde of biblical scholarship which says that what the Bible means is what it says to people in the places where they are hurting. But whatever we make of texts that Dr. Blair would be the first to admit are problematical, and whether or not we take issue with particular interpretations he proposes, we do well to ponder the central argument of his book.

Philip Blair believes that the discontent deep within us is born of the truth that we are far from home. We try to assuage that discontent by all manner of palliatives that at best offer some distraction but which necessarily leave us unsatisfied. There is no mending of our deepest needs within this present age, try as we may, try as we *must*, to make our days peaceful and our dealings just. But from beyond the rim of this fleeting world a star is rising promising a new dawn and the healing of our sorrows.

A century ago yet another writer sat at a desk before a window overlooking the Mediterranean. George MacDonald wrote these words:

Let us hold fast by our hopes. All colours are shreds of the rainbow. There is a rainbow of the cataract, of the paddle-wheel, of the falling wave; none of them is the rainbow, yet they are all of it; they all vanish but that which set them in their places and will set them again, the rainbow in the heart of God, vanishes never. Say not they are but hopes, for by our hopes we are saved.

Even so, come Lord Jesus.

John Pridmore

I: 'Centre of the World'

On 7 June 1967, as he stood beside the Wailing Wall in Jerusalem's Old City, Moshe Dayan announced, 'We have returned to our holiest of holy places, never to be parted from it again.' After fierce fighting from the commencement of the Six Day War, initiated by Israel two days earlier, Israeli forces had just wrested East Jerusalem from the Jordanians. Very soon a crudely lettered Hebrew sign appeared at the foot of the Wailing Wall proclaiming that the site was 'Beyt Knesseth', 'A Temple'. Then, in the face of international condemnation, the Old City was officially annexed to the Jewish state.

It was in 1949 that the Israeli cabinet first resolved that the city was 'an inseparable part of the State of Israel and its eternal capital'. Since then the Israeli stance has not wavered – up to the May 1999 election of Labour party leader Ehud Barak as Prime Minister, who declared in his victory speech that Jerusalem would remain 'united under our sovereignty for eternity – period'.

Early in 1995 the Israeli Housing Minister, Binyamin Ben-Eliezer, speaking in the context of the increasingly acrimonious Arab-Israeli peace talks, declared,

> The battle for Jerusalem has begun, and do not let anyone try and fool you. After the Six Day War, the Government decided on the unity of Jerusalem – and there is national consensus on this. Jerusalem is ours. We will do in it what we want, and we will rule as we see fit.

The following year, on 10 July 1996, the then Israeli Prime Minister Binyamin Netanyahu, fresh from his own election victory, told the US Congress to huge applause that he would never let Jerusalem be divided. Two days later the Israeli press was reporting what Mr Netanyahu had told the US leaders,' Israel will not compromise with respect to its demand that Palestinian institutions be closed in Jerusalem.' Faisal al-Husseini, top PLO official based at Orient House, a former hotel in Jerusalem serving as the PLO's unofficial 'Foreign Ministry', responded,

> To say that Jerusalem is not an issue for negotiations and no compromise . . . that is saying there is no peace. We have returned to the days of war.

The status of Jerusalem – Israel's 'eternal and indivisible' capital – is arguably the most critical issue of our day. Not for nothing was the city described in medieval times as 'the centre of the world'.

Catalyst of conflict

It is probable that the name Jerusalem is not of Hebrew origin. Most authorities are agreed that the final part of the word means 'peace'. The first part may mean 'possession' or 'foundation' though the cognate Assyrian language would give a meaning 'city of peace'. The salient fact about this ancient city, however, is that far from being a city of peace it has consistently been the catalyst of conflict.

Three world religions find a focus in Jerusalem. Throughout the long centuries of their dispersion in exile, Jews dreamed of a return to King David's capital and the Western Wall of Herod's Temple. Most Palestinians, being Muslims, on the other hand, have associated their struggle for national independence with the Al-Aqsa Mosque and the Dome of the Rock, whence Muhammad is believed to have ascended to heaven. The two shrines constitute, for Muslims, the third holiest places after Mecca and Medina. What is potentially so explosive about the situation is that Jewish Wall and Muslim Mosques are seamlessly, inextricably fused within 34 acres of ancient stonework that form part of the Old City. Jerusalem is, thirdly, a place of pilgrimage for Christians. The city and surrounding countryside boast many sites sacred to the memory of Jesus of Nazareth, founder of Christianity. The holiest spot of all is the Church of the Holy Sepulchre, again in the Old City; it is venerated by many Christians as the place where Jesus was crucified and buried.

Of all places on earth, Jerusalem most aptly illustrates the phenomenon of the 'eternal triangle'.

We find first mention of the city in cuneiform tablets discovered in 1887 by a peasant digging in the ruins of Tell al-Amarna in Egypt. These, believed to date from the fourteenth century B.C. (they could be older), are written in a dialect of Babylonian. At that time Jerusalem – 'Urusalim' in Babylonian – was ruled over by a king called Abdi-hepa, described in a letter of Shuwardata of Hebron to Pharaoh as 'a rogue'; it was then under the dominion of Egypt, being probably little more than a mountain fortress.

When the Israelites entered Canaan under Joshua (in the mid-thirteenth century B.C. according to most modern scholars though around 1400 B.C., or even earlier, in traditional chronology) Jerusalem was in the hands of the Jebusites, a Semitic tribe. Joshua did not take the city, possibly because of its extremely strong position, but when David became king in 1011/10 B.C. he found a surprise way into the citadel and overcame it, making Jerusalem instead of Hebron his capital.

Under David's immediate successors, the city was raided by Egyptians,

Philistines and Arabs. Then, in 587 B.C., when it was the capital of the southern kingdom of Judah (formed when ten of the Israelite tribes broke away from the rule of Solomon's son Rehoboam and established a separate northern kingdom, called Israel), the city and Temple were destroyed by Nebuchadrezzar of Babylon. The Persian king Cyrus captured Babylon in 539 B.C. and almost immediately gave permission for the Jews to return to their land and city and rebuild the Temple. The city walls, however, remained in ruins until Nehemiah restored them in the middle of the fifth century.

At the end of the fourth century Alexander the Great broke the power of Persia. Following his death one of his generals, Ptolemy, who founded the Ptolemaic dynasty in Egypt, entered Jerusalem and made it part of his kingdom. In 198 B.C. Palestine fell to the Seleucid king of Syria, Antiochus III. Thirty years later his successor Antiochus IV – who styled himself *Epiphanes* ('[God] manifest') – entered and plundered the city, destroying its walls and desecrating the Temple. His measures to hellenize Palestine included the prohibition of Jewish sacrifices in the Temple, and the erection of a Greek altar on the site of the old one on 25 December 167 B.C.

The Maccabean revolt led by Mattathiah and his sons – Judas Maccabeus, most prominently – resulted in the reconsecration of the Temple in 164 B.C.. Independence for Judea (as Judah became) was achieved, and the Hasmonean dynasty ruled a free Jerusalem until the middle of the first century. Roman generals and troops entered Jerusalem in 63 and 54 B.C., and a Parthian army plundered it in 40 B.C.. Three years later, Herod the Great, a Jew of Idumean descent, fought his way into the city and took control. He initiated an extensive building programme, including the rebuilding of the Temple on a lavish scale.

In A.D. 70, following the Jewish revolt against Rome which commenced in A.D. 66, the fortifications and Temple were destroyed by the armies of the Roman general Titus. Three towers were left standing, one of which, Phasael, still stands – incorporated in the present 'Tower of David'. After the second Jewish revolt of A.D. 132-135, led by Simeon Bar Kochba, the Roman Emperor Hadrian rebuilt Jerusalem (on a smaller scale) as a pagan city. All Jews were banished from the city. It was renamed Aelia Capitolina – after Jupiter Capitolinus, the god to whom it was dedicated.

Constantine, the Roman emperor who favoured Christianity early in the fourth century, allowed Jews to return to Jerusalem. The city now became Christian, churches and monasteries being built, including the Church of the Holy Sepulchre. But in 614 Persians stormed the city, destroying buildings, killing and taking prisoners. The Byzantine emperor recovered it, but in 637 it was taken by the Muslim Caliph Omar. In 691 the Caliph Abd al-Malik erected the Dome of the Rock on the Temple area, and this has stood there to this day.

Christians and Jews were treated with tolerance by the Muslims until semi-Barbarian Turks displaced the Arabs in the eleventh century.

In June 1099 the city fell to the Crusaders, amidst dreadful carnage, and the Latin kingdom of Jerusalem was proclaimed. Its first custodian, Godfrey of Bouillon, accepted the title of 'Defender of the Holy Sepulchre'. Defend it he did, defeating the first renewed Muslim challenge, in the form of an Egyptian army, as promptly as the following month. Godfrey died in July 1100 and was succeeded by Baldwin of Boulogne, who was crowned king of the new theocratic state on Christmas Day of that year. The Christian kingdom then settled down to its relatively peaceful though never very secure existence, disturbed periodically by influxes of pilgrims, and gaining some support from the recently founded military Orders of religion. Notwithstanding these Orders, nor the calling of new Crusades from time to time, Jerusalem fell to the Muslims in 1187. In 1229 the city and some other territories were restored to the Christians by the terms of a generous treaty between Sultan al-Kamil Muhammad of Egypt and the enigmatic 'Infidel Emperor' Frederick II – a lover of learning which included Arabic and Arab philosophy.

Jerusalem fell again to the Muslims in 1244, remaining in Egyptian hands almost continuously until 1517, when the Ottoman Turks took control, under Selim I. In 1542 the Sultan Suleiman the Magnificent rebuilt the city walls. The Turks held Palestine until the First World War, when it was conquered by British forces under General Allenby – whose task had been assisted by the 'Arab Revolt' in which T.E. Lawrence played a part. In 1917 – the year in which the Balfour Declaration declared the intentions of the British government to support the establishment of a national home for the Jewish people in Palestine – Allenby entered Jerusalem. As a result of their victories over the Turks in the War, the British received a mandate for the control of Palestine. This lasted from 1920 until 1948.

On 29 November 1947, the United Nations passed a resolution prescribing three things: the partition of Palestine into an Arab State and a Jewish State, the internationalisation of Jerusalem, and economic union of all three parts. The Jewish Agency (representing the Jews) accepted this plan, but the day following the UN decision the Arabs repudiated the resolution and launched a guerrilla war. When, on 14 May 1948, the British officially terminated their mandate, the Jewish National Council proclaimed the establishment of the State of Israel. On 15 May the combined armies of Egypt, Syria, Jordan, Lebanon, Iraq and Saudi Arabia invaded Israel. A truce was finally arranged on 7 January 1949, with Jerusalem straddling the armistice line. The walled Old City lay in the Hashemite kingdom of the Jordan, while the extensive western suburb was on the Israeli side.

The situation remained unchanged until the Six Day War of June 1967, when (as we have noted) the Old City was taken by the Israelis. Also taken at that time was the area of the Jordanian kingdom lying west of the River Jordan (the 'West Bank'), the Sinai desert (Egyptian territory), and the Golan Heights (Syrian territory). Finally, in 1978 Israel mounted a limited invasion of Lebanon and established a military presence along a strip of land to protect its own northern boundary (the 1949 armistice line with Lebanon). After its withdrawal following a second invasion of Lebanon in 1982, it again kept control of a chunk of southern Lebanese territory, which it called its 'Security Zone'. This was protected by the South Lebanon Army – a Christian militia trained, paid and controlled by Israel.

Focus for fanaticism

Fighting and destruction in and around the 'holy city' has been all too common over the centuries, yet seldom has there hung upon her situation as much as hangs on it today.

As so many times before, the issue of the city's status erupted into prominence in June 1998, when Israel announced a scheme to extend Jerusalem's municipal boundaries. Prime Minister Binyamin Netanyahu won cabinet approval for the plan, which Palestinian leaders said amounted to a *de facto* annexation of territories supposed to be subject to final status negotiations between the two sides. The creation of this 'greater Jerusalem' involves the incorporation westwards of Israeli commuter towns, but more controversially the forming of an 'umbrella municipality' over parts of the West Bank beyond the 1967 Green Line to the south, east and north, to include eight Jewish settlements. The plan was prompted, it appears, by the desire to alter the demographic balance of Jews and Arabs within the municipality so that the latter did not become at some future date a majority.

A spokesman for the Palestinians told Israel radio, 'It's a total violation of the Oslo agreement.' The American State Department called the decision 'extremely provocative', but later softened its criticism; the European Union said the plan would 'complicate the peace process'. Mr Netanyahu protested that there had been a campaign to distort the decision, which was 'entirely municipal, entirely administrative, with no political implications'.

Three weeks later the UN Security Council told Israel not to act on its decision, but the Jewish state merely responded that the latter could not intervene. The Palestinian Authority then, in effect, retaliated – with a step to expand its status in the UN. A vote was passed authorising the Palestinians, though still non-voting, to join in General Assembly debates, sponsor resolutions and take part in conferences.

In such ways the issue of Jerusalem – above all others – continually frustrates the Middle East peace process.

Jerusalem is a city of around 630,000 inhabitants – some 29% of them Palestinians occupying East Jerusalem. Excluding the above artificial extension of its boundaries, the municipality covers an area of 123 square kilometres (47.4 square miles). It is not large by modern standards, yet the eyes of approaching a third of the world's population – Jews, Muslims, Christians – are focused on it. The more fanatical of these have sworn their readiness to die fighting for its preservation as a shrine of their religion or ideology. Deeds speak louder than words, but in recent years there have been plenty of people prepared to back their words with deeds.

The conflict over Jerusalem is, in fact, merely the wider Arab-Israeli struggle writ small. And that struggle is not simply between the *Arabs* and Israel. One of the loudest voices pledging support for the 'freedom of Palestine' has been that of Iran.

At the end of 1992 Ibrahim Gosheh, spokesman for Hamas, the militant Islamic movement, announced that Iran had promised financial and political support for 'the war to liberate Palestine'. Iran has been as good as her word. US intelligence for long claimed that Palestinian suicide bombers operating in Israel were receiving their training in Iran. This was corroborated by Israeli police in May 1996 when they announced that a man who had prematurely set off a bomb in Jerusalem the previous month had been equipped by Iranian handlers with plastic explosives and sent from Iran to Israel to carry out bombings.

According to a report by Con Coughlin (*The Daily Telegraph*, 7 July 1996), Iran has established at least 11 camps throughout the country in order to train terrorists for operations around the world, an estimated 5,000 volunteers passing through the camps each year. Some are devoted to training specific groups of foreign nationals, like Nahavand camp in the Iranian town of Hamadan, which is used exclusively by Lebanon's Hizbollah Islamic fundamentalist group, or the Fateh Ghani Husseini camp at Qom, mainly used by Turkish Islamic militants. According to US intelligence, Iran also trains and funds Islamic rebels in Algeria, organises terrorist schooling in Sudan, and has supported Hizbollah financially to the tune of many millions of dollars. Hamas, of course, works in close collusion with Hizbollah, fulfilling a 1992 pledge that it would strengthen its ties with this pro-Iranian militant movement based in south Lebanon.

Despite the recent apparent thaw in US-Iran relationships, in May 1998 a senior official of the US State Department told reporters, 'Terrorist activity directed from Iran has continued into 1998.' The Department claimed that, despite Iran's election of a more moderate president, Mohammed Khatami, in August 1997, Iran had been 'the most active sponsor of state terrorism' in 1997, with Iranian agents responsible for 'at least 13 assassinations'. It pointed out that leaders of various terrorist organisations had gathered in Tehran in the fall of 1997 to discuss enhanced co-ordination and seek more funds.

In an article arguing the need for the West to maintain its intelligence capability intact in the post-Cold War era (*The Times Higher Education Supplement*, 14 November 1997), Christopher Andrew, professor of modern and contemporary history at Cambridge University, describes Iran as 'the most dangerous rogue regime' in the world. He cites the fact that President Rafsanjani boasted in 1995 that Iran had completed the first stage in the production of a nuclear bomb, and that 'both the CIA and Israeli intelligence calculate that, within 18 months, Iran will have nuclear missiles with a range long enough to reach Israel'. A more conservative timescale for Iranian attainment of nuclear capability was announced in March 1996 by the Washington Institute of Near East Policy; it estimated 'ten years or less'. The Institute said that Iran had amassed up to 2,000 tons of chemical weapons and already had missiles capable of hitting major cities in the Middle East.

Iran's physical tentacles spread far; her sphere of influence is even wider. She has established herself in the eyes of devout Muslims everywhere as the bastion of unadulterated Islamic belief and practice in the face of 'decadent' Western culture. The pro-Western government of Hosni Mubarak of Egypt has accordingly been threatened by Iranian sponsored violence, following an order by the mullahs in February 1993 for fundamentalist organisations on Iran's payroll to topple the Mubarak regime. The unsuccessful assassination attempt by Islamic extremists on Mubarak in Addis Ababa on 26 June 1995, responsibility for which was claimed by Egypt's main revolutionary Islamic group Gamaa al-Islamiya (which vowed it would yet kill him), was believed by Western intelligence to have had the support of Sudan, and in particular of Sudan's militant Islamic leader Hassan al-Turabi, who has close links with Iran.

Tehran has found in Sudan a replacement for Lebanon as a fertile nursery for would-be terrorists, and it is estimated that at any time 3,000 of Iran's Revolutionary Guards are resident in the country – officially as 'military advisers'. Sudan's regime, which in 1989 seized power under

General Omar Hassan al-Bashir in a coup supported by the National Islamic Front, and has carried on a ruthless war against its own southern rebels, has accordingly played host to such Middle Eastern and North African terrorist organisations as Hamas, Hizbollah, both the Egyptian and Jordanian chapters of the Islamic Brotherhood, the Tunisian al-Nahda and the Algerian Armed Islamic Group. Further, Sudan's own Mujahidin have fanned across the region, having been found in such far off places as Bosnia and Kashmir. In July 1995 Sudan's Minister of State for Foreign Affairs, acknowledging that members of Hamas were resident in Khartoum, declared, 'These people are not terrorists, they are freedom fighters.'

There have from time to time been indications that Iran might conclude a diplomatic reconciliation with Iraq, bringing to an end the enmity that created the long and costly Gulf War of 1980-88. There have also been signs of warmer relations with Syria; the two countries have had a long-standing strategic alliance, but have tended to compete for influence over Lebanon's Hizbollah resistance movement. Two factors have been of particular relevance in bringing these nations closer: the strengthening of Turkish-Israeli ties, especially military co-operation, and the near-collapse of the Arab-Israeli peace process. Both developments have encouraged the governments of all three countries – Iran, Iraq and Syria – to form a united front against Israeli, Turkish and American policies.

Saddam Hussein of Iraq still talks as if he is a latter-day Nebuchadrezzar, who will one day – like that earlier Babylonian tyrant – crush the nation of Israel. In July 1998, following the claim by UN arms inspectors that Iraq had been arming missile warheads with deadly VX gas during the 1991 Gulf War, the regime issued an unequivocal statement: it demanded an immediate and unconditional lifting of UN sanctions, then went on to call for a 'clear strategy' to deal with Israel, 'the usurpers of the land of Palestine and its holy places and the killers of its people'. If such a strategy were not implemented the world could expect what the regime had already warned of – 'a great Jihad'.

By the end of 1998 it looked as if the Iraqi dictator had effectively won his long and determined effort to stalemate UN inspectors searching for hidden weapons of mass destruction. A body blow to the UN effort was the resignation in August 1998 of Scott Ritter, one of the top inspectors, who said the monitoring had been neutralised by the Iraqis some time previously. In November Saddam Hussein's intransigence brought matters to a head; the UN inspectors were recalled and a few days later US and British planes were on the brink of launching punitive bombing raids on Iraq when at the very last minute the Iraqi leader backed down and the allied attack was aborted. The inspectors immediately returned, yet within a week Iraq was again being confrontational over the surrender of documents. The USA, backed by Britain, announced that air attacks might be launched at any moment, without warning, and on December 16 – two days after President Clinton had paid an historic goodwill visit to Palestinian Gaza – operation Desert Fox began, with first missiles and then bombs raining down on selected Iraqi targets.

The Iraqi leader's reaction was to denounce a 'Zionist conspiracy' and vow that there would be 'no compromise' in his country's response. On December 19, however, Clinton called a halt to the air strikes, maintaining that strategic objectives had been fulfilled. Saddam Hussein duly announced that Iraq had been 'crowned with victory' – a claim that did not seem wholly empty as tens of thousands protested their sympathy with Iraq in demonstrations across the Arab world (in Palestine, above all), and the realisation dawned in the West that the attacks had not only exposed deep divisions over Iraq in the UN Security Council but also given the regime precisely the excuse it needed finally and irrevocably to expel the UN Special Commission (UNSCOM). It was far from certain, furthermore, that the bombing had achieved its goal of 'degrading' the country's capacity to manufacture weapons of mass destruction.

Saddam Hussein's claim to have won the day was given further substance by the admission of US intelligence services (the CIA) in March 1999 that for three years they had – just as the Iraqi leader had protested – been infiltrating agents and espionage equipment into UN arms control teams without UNSCOM's knowledge in order to spy on the Iraqi military. The revelation of these activities (forbidden in terms of UNSCOM's brief) caused the Arab League to swing behind the Iraqi regime as it demanded, together with China, an end to US/British bombing in the exclusion zones, prompted Russia and France to be critical and furnished the dictator himself with a powerful argument for the removal of sanctions – leaving the USA and Britain isolated in the UN Security Council in their hard-line approach to Iraq; by June 1999 even Britain recommended the lifting of sanctions if Baghdad answered certain questions on its weapons' programme. Meanwhile, both bombing and sanctions are opposed by aid workers on humanitarian grounds and Scott Ritter, none other, concludes in a new book that the single solution to the 'Iraq problem' is accommodation with Saddam, the rehabilitation of his regime (*Endgame: Solving the Iraq Problem – Once and for All*, Simon and Schuster, 1999). In Alistair Cooke's words (*Letter from America*, 7 March 1999, B.B.C.), 'Saddam Hussein is declared the winner.'

Despite his country's poverty, largely the result of UN sanctions, Saddam Hussein has pressed on with expensive building projects on the site of ancient Babylon, as well as the construction of a vast palace (its Italian marble alone costing $24 million) on the banks of the Tigris in

Baghdad. Political dissidence has been crushed by summary and arbitrary executions, while the common people have been cowed by routine torture and ferociously cruel penalties against petty crime. The marshes in the south have mostly been drained, with thousands of families forcibly removed (many villagers being murdered) to facilitate military operations against Shi'ite opponents. The survival technique of a dictator who has lived through two Gulf wars, punitive raids, bloody rebellions, coup plots and assassination attempts, has been described by an Iraqi businessmen, 'He has fostered the myth of his invincibility by moving against his enemies before they even think of moving against him.'

Saddam Hussein is an astute politician, adept at winning the support of fellow Arabs. In January 1993 Yasser Arafat visited Baghdad and met him. The Iraqi leader offered Arafat $50 million to cover the deficit of UNRWA (the UN agency that looks after Palestinian refugees), decorated him with the 'Order of the Mother of All Battles', as a tribute to the Palestinian people's stand alongside the Iraqi people and armed forces in the 1991 Gulf War, and advised him to press on with peace talks with Israel.

Ultimate impasse

Those 'talks' were at a virtual standstill on 17 May 1999, when Ehud Barak won his landslide victory over Binyamin Netanyahu in the Israeli leadership election. There was immediate talk – in Israel, across the Arab world and in Western capitals – of a resumption of peace negotiations and swift progress towards a final settlement of the 'Palestinian problem'. Mr Barak, a former chief of general staff in the Israeli army, who is nevertheless said greatly to admire the first century pragmatist Rabbi Johanan ben Zakkai (see below), certainly let it be known that things would be different. Declaring that he wished to be leader of every member of his nation (Arabs constitute over 17% of Israel's six million population), he phoned Yasser Arafat the day after his triumph to pledge his readiness to work for peace. Washington, meanwhile, had already set a target of one year for a settlement.

There was another side to the picture, however. Throughout his election campaign, Mr Barak was vague about what he intended to do. He set a one-year target for bringing Israeli troops out of southern Lebanon, but he did not explain how he would proceed with the Palestinians. Commenting on the election result, the secretary-general of the Arab League was non-committal, 'Barak has said he supports peace but we want to see what he is going to do.' Such caution was well-founded: Mr Barak abstained in a cabinet vote on the Oslo accords during the government of Yitzhak Rabin and as well as vowing not to surrender

East Jerusalem he has stated that major Jewish West Bank settlements will remain under Israeli control. While accepting the concept of 'land for peace' and contemplating withdrawal from the Golan Heights in exchange for a settlement with Syria (and Hizbollah), his position on a future Palestinian state is different in tone rather than substance from that of his predecessor. An overriding issue, one on which he knows he has to deliver, is that of Israel's security. Meanwhile, the ultra-Orthodox Shas party, hardline on religious issues, gained 17 seats (up from 10) in the 120-seat Knesset, the right-wing Michael Kleiner, instrumental in bringing down the Netanyahu coalition, has warned that 'half the nation' will take to the streets in protest if more land is given up and, on a different flank, Sheikh Ahmed Yassin, founder and spiritual leader of Islamic Hamas, has given notice that attacks against Israel will continue regardless of the change in leadership.

In order to appreciate the pressures faced by Israeli leaders of any political persuasion, as well as by the Palestinian leadership, let us trace the recent course of the 'peace process'.

The October 1998 Wye Plantation summit in USA produced an agreement whereby the Israelis would withdraw from a further 13% of the West Bank, to add to the 3% previously fully vacated (and 26% partially), in return for security guarantees from the Palestinians. Yet the guarantees demanded of Yasser Arafat by Binyamin Netanyahu were so tight as to be almost impossible of fulfilment. The Palestinian leader's position became, as a result, increasingly untenable.

The election of Netanyahu's government in 1996 placed Mr Arafat in a position of considerable delicacy. There were always Palestinians who were opposed to the PLO leader and his policy of an accommodation with Israel, his readiness to accept, in the 1993 Oslo accords, a mere shadow of the original dream of 'complete liberation'. Such believed he was negotiating from a position of impossible weakness and was throwing away the legitimacy enshrined in UN resolutions, particularly resolutions 242, 338 and 425, the basis of the Madrid 1991 peace conference, which called for the return of occupied land for peace. They considered he was destroying the PLO, in which they had found an identity and a national voice. Now their fears are close to being realised.

There are approaching two million Palestinians in the West Bank and over a million in Gaza, 3.05 million in all. There is high unemployment, particularly in Gaza, where well over a third of employable people are looking for work. Initially, the majority of Palestinians believed the Oslo accords with Israel would deliver a measure of prosperity along with the promise of peace, yet in fact most have become poorer. Incomes, buying power and private investment have plunged while the number of families living in poverty has swollen. Many Palestinians are now losing faith in the peace process as their hopes for prosperity fade. According to polls, support is increasing for Hamas leader Sheikh Ahmed Yassin. Placing the latter under house arrest and apprehending 100 other Hamas activists (as Arafat did in October 1998) has hardly diminished such support.

There is much criticism of Arafat's repressive, dictatorial methods. Said Aburish, author of the book *Arafat: from Defender to Dictator* (Bloomsbury, 1998), had this to say when interviewed by the B.B.C. in September 1998,

> He's not fit to govern. . . . He's surrounded himself with a collection of corrupt people. . . . Why should we accommodate him and put half of our people in prison, so to speak? His record on human rights is deplorable. He doesn't care. Everything is still in his hands. Everybody supports the *promise* of the peace process, but the promise hasn't been fulfilled.

Mr Arafat has tried to fight back by playing tough on the world stage. In September 1998 he floated the idea of unilaterally declaring an independent Palestinian state on 4 May 1999, when the Oslo agreement was originally scheduled to be concluded; he then challenged the United Nations to support such a declaration. Mr Netanyahu commented, 'We could each decide unilaterally what we each want, and we'd have an explosion.'

In December 1998, the Israeli Foreign Minister Ariel Sharon – founder of Netanyahu's Likud party and on record as having said that Yasser Arafat should be tried as a 'war criminal' – was more explicit, warning that if Arafat carried out his threat Israel would have to annexe parts of the West Bank. The process has in effect begun, with Israeli West Bank settlers following Sharon's advice (in the wake of the Wye agreement) to 'grab the hilltops' in anticipation of final status talks.

The Likud government's tough stance sprang from its power base. Mr Netanyahu's 1996 election victory was in large measure due to the spate of devastating Hamas suicide bomb attacks mounted in Israel early in the year, the 20% lead in the polls of the more moderate Mr Shimon Peres, who succeeded Mr Yitzhak Rabin as Prime Minister after the latter's assassination in November 1995, being gradually whittled away.

Once elected, Mr Netanyahu was under pressure from the Right to take a hard line in the peace negotiations, within days appointing Ariel Sharon to a post having responsibility for 'political and security areas'. Mr Sharon had supervised a drive taking 120,000 Jewish settlers to the West Bank and the Gaza Strip between 1977 and 1984, instigated the military invasion of Lebanon in 1983, and opposed the Oslo agreements. In his new post he set about organising the building of roads connecting

Jewish West Bank settlements with Israel.

Pressure was also brought on Mr Netanyahu after his victory by religious parties. The new Prime Minister had no option but to heed their voice, since he needed their support, as he had needed their votes, to secure a clear majority for his new administration. Within a week of the election Jewish settlers were gathering before the Tomb of the Patriarchs in the centre of Hebron to celebrate the 'miracle' of the electoral victory – for which they had earnestly prayed – of the man who during his campaign had said, 'Jews have a right to settle anywhere and everywhere in the Land of Israel'.

There are now approaching 370,000 Israeli settlers established across the pre-1967 war ceasefire line separating Israel from the West Bank and Gaza Strip – over 180,000 in annexed East Jerusalem, a similar number in the West Bank and nearly 6,000 in Gaza. These inhabit some 180 settlements, linked by highways. Further, there are 17,000 settlers in the Golan Heights, where the recent building of a 220-room hotel, as a gesture of solidarity with the settlers, is a measure of how permanent the settlements were always meant to be; they were 'facts on the ground', designed to pre-empt future negotiation.

At the end of the five-year interim period of Palestinian autonomy set by the Oslo accords, on 4 May 1999 (when Arafat, under pressure from Clinton, refrained from declaring an independent state), the Palestinian Authority found itself in control of just 10% of the West Bank – or less than 30% including villages where the Israeli army is responsible for security and free to search and enter, destroy houses and make arrests – and two-thirds of Gaza. Furthermore, the area over which it ruled comprised scattered enclaves, with Israeli roads and/or checkpoints dividing one from another.

An Israeli withdrawal from all the territories occupied in 1967, as demanded at the Cairo summit of Arab leaders in June 1996, is not on the cards, whatever the rights and wrongs of the case. With the exception perhaps of the Golan Heights, further withdrawal is likely to involve only those areas that have no significant settlements and which do not constitute a security threat. Beyond all, of course, looms the question of Jerusalem.

After Mr Netanyahu had, during that visit to America in 1996, vowed not to allow Jerusalem ever again to be divided, Mr Arafat, from his own presidential seat in tiny Gaza, curtly retorted, 'Al-Quds al-Sharif [holy Jerusalem] is the capital of Palestine forever.'

Jerusalem constitutes the final, seemingly unsurmountable hurdle to peace – an ultimate impasse. The issue of its status transcends all others because it is 'holy'. The Jerusalem problem is a *religious* problem.

Religion, politics, war and peace

Religion frequently encourages prejudice, intolerance and violence.

Muslim extremism is just one religious stance illustrating this statement. Islamic fundamentalism presupposes and teaches that the greatest service a man can do for God is that of fighting his 'enemies' – blasphemers of various kinds. He may do so by employing argument, certainly, but where necessary he must use the sword. Martyrdom is coveted as the supreme goal, for it is believed to ensure divine pardon for past sins and guarantee an immediate entry into paradise – a *special* paradise, indeed, according to promises given by Hamas clerics to prospective suicide bombers, in which the crowned martyr will enjoy the attentions of seventy-two virgin brides, with places reserved also for members of his family.

Thus it is that more and more terrorist acts are performed by such bombers. A particularly horrifying atrocity was perpetrated by the driver – observed smiling as he approached his death – of the truck that exploded in Beirut in 1983, destroying the American Marine barracks and killing 241 people. Or there was the bus attack carried out by the 27-year-old Palestinian who, in the name of Hamas, killed himself and 21 Israelis in Tel Aviv on 19 October 1994. In a pre-recorded video he stated, 'If our demands are not met we will continue heroic operations, and there are many young people who are ready for martyrdom for God's sake.'

The ripples of fundamentalist extremism have spread outwards from the main centres in the last few years and now affect a number of other Arab nations – such as Egypt (many hundreds killed in the cycle of Islamic extremism and reprisals by security forces), Jordan, Algeria (an estimated 100,000 killed in the government's war against extremists), Tunisia and Bahrain. Even Libya has been affected, clashes having erupted in Benghazi between security forces and Islamic militants. Colonel Gaddafi may be fiercely anti-Zionist and have a reputation for fathering terrorism, but he is a severe critic of fundamentalist 'heretics'.

Nor are the ravages of militant Islamic fundamentalism confined to countries within the Arab world. Muslim inspired violence is increasing further afield: in Turkey, Afghanistan, India, Pakistan, Indonesia and the Philippines, for example.

It is pious sentiment, too, that has for the most part fired Jewish individuals who have perpetrated acts of violence. Most appalling was the dawn massacre of 54 Arab Muslims in the Tomb of the Patriarchs, or 'Abraham's Mosque' (sacred to Jews and Muslims alike), in Hebron on 25 February 1994. This was carried out by Baruch Goldstein, an American-born doctor from the nearby settlement of Kiryat Arba, described by associates as a 'religious' man; after spraying the worshippers with automatic fire, Goldstein was himself killed. Or we could cite – in some ways equally terrible – the assassination of Mr Yitzhak Rabin on 4 November 1995.

Like Islamic suicide bombers, Yigal Amir claimed to act in God's name when he killed the Israeli Prime Minister. He told an Israeli court the day after the atrocity that he had acted alone, but 'maybe with God's help'. Jewish law, he explained, prescribed death for anyone who 'turns over his people and the land to the enemy'. Later, when about to be sentenced to life imprisonment on 27 March 1996, he repeated the claim, 'I did what I did for God, the people of Israel and the Torah.' (*Cf.* Karpin, M. and I. Friedman, *Murder in the Name of God: The Plot to Kill Yitzhak Rabin*, Granta, 1999).

But can it really be *religious* sentiment that prompts such killings, whether by Muslims, or Jews, or members of other religious groups? The answer is that throughout the world acts of violence are continuously being perpetrated in the name of Islam, Judaism (or 'Zionism'), Hinduism, Buddhism, even Christianity – as well as in the name of countless sects. We cannot say whether the claim to be acting in the name of God, as he is understood in those religions, is sincere; motives are never fully ascertainable, and many use religion as a cloak for personal anger, vindictiveness or cruelty.

With regard to Islam, there is Koranic authority for the concept of Jihad, or 'holy war'. Islam is essentially theocratic; it encompasses the whole of life, including mankind's corporate life, which is politics. And politics involves wielding the sword.

Judaism is also theocratic, and therefore political, as originally defined in the Hebrew scriptures (the Old Testament) – especially in its first five books, containing the Torah, or Mosaic Law. Possession of the land of Canaan, or 'promised land', was part of the contract God made with the sons of Jacob/Israel, who were commanded to *fight* for their territory. When, centuries later, they lost it to the Romans, a new and necessarily more spiritual form of Judaism was born. They had not only lost the land; more importantly they had lost the Temple. Animal sacrifices were no longer possible, so another form of 'sacrifice' had to be found. Rabbi Johanan ben Zakkai, who escaped from Jerusalem shortly before it fell to the Romans in A.D. 70, taught that this must be the sacrifice of kindness, prayer, almsgiving and general piety, centred upon synagogue worship.

Rabbi Zakkai's version of Judaism has its modern adherents. The ultra-Orthodox Jewish sect called Netura Karta, for example, opposes a political expression of Judaism, like Zionism, on the grounds that it is blasphemous to establish a Jewish state before the advent of Messiah. The sect even made a pact with Yasser Arafat, in whom they saw an ally.

The majority of Jews today, however, including Orthodox rabbis from Israel and elsewhere, support the broad aims of Zionism. Indeed, some religious Zionists go further: they regard occupied territory as part of Eretz Israel – the biblical land of Israel – and not on any account to be surrendered. On 12 July 1995 Zionist rabbis, including a former Chief Rabbi, having already told Israeli troops to defy orders to evacuate the 135,000 Jewish settlers, issued a religious law in defiance of the policy of Mr Rabin's government: they announced that it was unlawful for soldiers to vacate their West Bank bases. The rabbinical ruling caused turmoil, putting religiously minded soldiers in an impossible dilemma.

Mr Rabin's assassin, as we have seen, had a religious agenda. To Yigal Amir, as to every religious Jew, bringing Messiah and so achieving the redemption of the world is linked to possessing the land. Giving back the land to the Palestinians – as Rabin and Peres suggested – is like throwing a gift back in God's face, for *the holiest thing in Jewish religion is the land*.

'Religious' Jews and 'fundamentalist' Muslims striving to attain their respective political goals, nationhood centred on Jerusalem, are both pursuing the age-old quest for the kingdom of God on earth – the Millennium, the New Jerusalem. The tragedy is that their two visions are incompatible. This is seen most starkly over the issue of the Temple, the rebuilding of which – according to a prominent Israeli journalist interviewed by the B.B.C. for the series *Crisis in the House of David* (1998) – is the ultimate goal of even quite moderate Jews. As we have noted, the Western Wall of Herod's Temple (the third to be built) and two of the holiest Mosques are 'seamlessly, inextricably fused' in Jerusalem's Old City.

What of the third element in the 'eternal triangle', of which Jerusalem is the focus? What of Christianity?

The Christian Church – without support from its scriptures – has also adopted a political role. In an earlier book (*What On Earth? The Church in the World and the Call of Christ,* Lutterworth, 1993), I show how the Church first 'entered politics' after the Emperor Constantine accepted Christianity early in the fourth century; how, in the Middle Ages, the Western (Catholic) Church raised armies for Crusades to wrest Jerusalem from the Muslim infidel, going on to claim supreme political authority on earth; how – notwithstanding the protest against the 'church political' by Luther and other sixteenth century reformers – the Church has, in the nineteenth and twentieth centuries, laid increasing emphasis on the idea that Christ's very message is political. I describe how the World Council of Churches (representing world Protestantism) has encouraged and supported violent revolutionary movements throughout the world for at least three decades, and how the Roman Catholic Church has recently been strengthening its political role.

The Roman Catholic Church has been keen to enhance its political stature since recognizing afresh the expediency of its time-honoured strategy of wielding temporal power the better to advance its 'spiritual' aims. It is doing so, largely, by increasing and strengthening its network of diplomatic missions worldwide. It has opened a number of new Papal nunciatures, especially in Eastern Europe, and in 1994 restored diplomatic relations with Israel. Pope John Paul II, the most political Pope of modern times (*cf.* Willey, David, *God's Politician: John Paul at the Vatican*, Faber, 1992), has in particular sought to shape events by pronouncing on issues of the day – especially those relating to war, and peace.

'Peace' is in fact the main burden of the Church's current message to the world. Addressing pilgrims and tourists in St Peter's Square on 7 May 1995, the fiftieth anniversary of the ending of the Second World War in Europe, the Pontiff warned people 'to reject the culture of war and to seek every legitimate and opportune means to seek an end to conflicts.' His 1998 Christmas Day message referred, among other things, to his hopes for 'measures to halt the production and sale of arms . . . to restrain the bloodied hand of those responsible for genocide and crimes of war'. His homily issued for World Peace Day, 1 January 1999, had a slightly different approach, though displaying a like preoccupation with social and political issues: it focused on human rights violations, of which the global free market economy was identified as a primary source. Such violations, John Paul declared, sow 'the seeds of instability, rebellion and violence', making the most urgent need 'a new vision of global progress in solidarity'. Dr Carey, Archbishop of Canterbury, has made similar pronouncements, his message to representatives of over 50 nations gathered in St Paul's Cathedral for the 1995 anniversary of the War being that 'as political or religious leaders it is our duty to continue to seek the way of peace for this and future generations'. Conspicuous by its absence in such pontifical or episcopal utterances is reference to Christ's offer of spiritual peace to the individual.

Sometimes the Church seeks to intervene in situations of conflict, as in the Gulf War of early 1991 (see below), or over the 1999 Kosovo crisis. As regards the latter, the Pope joined the World Council of Churches in urging Nato and Yugoslavia to halt military action over the Western and Orthodox periods of Easter, then, on a visit in early May to Romania, second centre after Russia for the Orthodox Church, issued a joint declaration with the Orthodox patriarch calling on all sides to lay down their arms and seek peace.

The 'imperative of peace' between peoples and nations is deemed by today's churchmen to be sufficient ground for almost any act of progressive change. In June 1995, Prince Hassan of Jordan became the first non-Christian to preach in Oxford's Christ Church Cathedral (founded in the sixteenth century), and the first Muslim to preach in any English cathedral. The Dean of Christ Church defended his decision to extend the invitation by citing among other things the Prince's peace-making activities in the Middle East. In the same month, Roman Catholic bishops joined Muslim religious leaders and diplomats for inaugural worship in Rome's first mosque – furnishing the Pope with an opportunity to call for freedom of worship for Christians living in Muslim lands. And, at a memorial service in St Paul's Cathedral for King Hussein of Jordan in July 1999, to honour in particular his commitment to peace, a reading from the Koran included an assertion incompatible with the Christian Gospel.

Today's Church has largely followed the path taken by strict Muslims and pious Jews: pursuit of an earthly kingdom, through political – and thus sometimes violent – means.

The Pontiff, Palestine, and a New Jerusalem

How has this politicised Church, calling for a new world order of peace and goodwill, responded to the situation in the Middle East, and in particular to the problem of Palestine?

The Christian Church finds itself, as we have seen, at the very heart of the Arab-Israeli conflict. For its founder was crucified just outside Jerusalem, and the building commemorating that event is in today's Old City. There are now about 15,000 Christians living in Jerusalem – most of them Palestinian, the rest foreign clergy and officials. These, and other surviving Christian communities in Israel and the occupied territories (totalling some 130,000 and 40,000 Christians respectively), are currently facing a new challenge.

In cities like Gaza, Nablus and Hebron, as well as in East Jerusalem, Christians have been targeted by Muslims. Violence is rare, but many Christian Palestinians talk about being exiles in their own land, finding their social status diminished and opportunities for good jobs or promotion increasingly rare. The result has been a steady exodus from Palestine to Lebanon, or further afield to North America or other Western countries. Following one incident in Jerusalem's Old City in 1995, when Christian youths were attacked by a group of young Muslims, a senior Israeli official commented, 'Christians are caught in the middle, trying to protect their own interests without provoking their fellow Arabs, and afraid of appearing too close to Israel.'

'Caught in the middle . . . trying to protect their own interests.' The phrases perfectly sum up the stance of the wider Church in relation to the Arab-Israeli conflict – as also, in many respects, to its attitude to other conflicts involving Muslims. Church leaders, mostly concerned about the *material* welfare of their flocks, have devoted themselves to a delicate balancing act, wary of offending those likely to retaliate.

The Church's deportment in relation to the 1991 Gulf War is instructive. Pope John Paul opposed the offensive against Iraq to liberate Kuwait, claiming that Western powers had not exhausted diplomatic attempts to resolve the conflict, and that the force used was excessive. His efforts to seek peace and reconciliation were such that he was rewarded by a letter of salutation from the Secretary-General of the Islamic Conference. When the war was over, the Pontiff, at an Extraordinary Summit, went so far as to announce that 'for years already war has been excluded as a means of solving conflicts'.

The response of world Protestantism to the Gulf War was similar: the Seventh Assembly of the World Council of Churches marked its conclusion on 20 February 1991 by calling for an immediate and unconditional ceasefire, as well as the convening of a Peace Conference on the Middle East.

The position adopted by the Pope in relation to the Bosnian conflict in former Yugoslavia differed from his stance over the Gulf War. On 23 January 1994, the day after a Serbian mortar attack had killed six children in Sarajevo, he declared, 'Appropriate authorities have the responsibility to try everything humanly possible to disarm the aggressor and create conditions for a just and lasting peace.' With these words he was apparently blessing the use of force. That this was his meaning was indicated by the fact that a senior Vatican spokesman had, earlier that month, spoken of the Holy See supporting 'precise, proportionate and perhaps demonstrative' military action if all other efforts failed.

Despite – or perhaps because of – their incipient fears of Islamic aggression, church leaders have been active in seeking solutions to the problems of the Middle East.

At the Extraordinary Summit held at the Vatican in March 1991, it was affirmed that the primary orientations of the Roman Catholic Church in its work in the Middle East included the need to find solutions for the Palestinian problem, the situation in Lebanon, and the Kurdish and Cypriot problems. Sometimes the Pope involves himself personally. In May 1997 John Paul visited the Lebanon, where he celebrated the Mass before a huge crowd. In his address the Pontiff spoke of the need for (political) peace. A student onlooker commented, 'The Pope's visit and the Mass was not just for Christians, but for the whole people of the country.' She predicted that a second visit would 'bring peace to the country'.

Meanwhile, the Pope plans to visit Jerusalem, Nazareth and Bethlehem in March 2000.

The Anglican Church has been equally active. In April 1991 a gathering of the Primates of the Anglican Communion reaffirmed a 1988 Lambeth Conference resolution on the West Bank and Gaza; the resolution recognised both the existence of Israel and the rights of Palestinians to self-determination. In 1992 Dr Carey, Archbishop of Canterbury, followed this up by embarking on a kind of peace mission, meeting members of the Jordanian and Israeli governments and representatives of the Palestinian community. In conference with the Israeli Prime Minister, he broached the question of Palestinian political and human rights.

Whether or not the Church is even-handed in its peacebroking efforts worldwide, there is no denying the earnestness with which it fulfils this new, self-appointed role – a role which could lead to an interesting opportunity.

The nearest thing to an Israeli proposal for a Palestinian Jerusalem has probably been an idea floated by Israeli negotiators (reported in the Israeli press in May 1996) for a 'second, Palestinian Jerusalem' to rise alongside the Israeli-controlled city. Sir Martin Gilbert, author of *Jerusalem in the Twentieth Century* (Chatto and Windus, 1996) outlined a similar idea in an article in *The Daily Telegraph* (23 April 1996), but he offered further a possible solution to the 'religious' problem constituted by the city. He wrote,

> Thirty years ago, a distinguished Israeli civil servant Walter Eytan proposed that the Muslim holy places, including the Dome and the Al-Aqsa Mosque, could be transferred to Muslim sovereignty. With Muslim sovereignty over the Muslim holy places, Arafat could thus 'rule' both over the Dome (though he would have to reach an agreement with King Hussein about this), and also over areas which are in sight of the Dome, which are not part of 'undivided' Jerusalem of the Israeli perspective, yet are very much part of the urban area of greater Jerusalem.

It was perhaps something along these lines that was in the mind of Mr Shimon Peres in July 1994 when, as Israeli Foreign Minister, he announced,

> I have said Jerusalem is closed politically and open religiously. This means that it will remain unified, and only as Israel's capital, not two capitals. It will remain under Israeli sovereignty. However, if it comes to the needs and rights of the various believers, we are open to proposals.

His remarks, indicating a subtle shift in Israeli strategy, were apparently prompted by a comment by King Hussein that only God can have sovereignty over Jerusalem's holy places. One thought led to another: Israel had recently forged full diplomatic ties with the Vatican: perhaps (Mr Peres is reported to have mused aloud) the Holy See could act as mediator.

Whether the Vatican was approached on the matter at the time we do not know, but it quickly took a practical step towards assuming the role envisaged by Mr Peres. On 25 October 1994 it announced that it had agreed to establish 'official relations' with the PLO, with the latter setting up an 'office of representation' at the Holy See. Another step – in a way – was the publication in October 1994 of Pope John Paul's book on the future of mankind, *Crossing the Threshold of Hope* (Jonathan Cape), described by Vatican spokesman Dr Navarro-Valls as 'not a testament but a programme'. In it, the Pontiff spoke of his hopes for 'a new world, a new Europe and a new civilisation'.

Are such hopes, echoing those expressed three years earlier by another world leader and reiterated in John Paul's 1998 encyclical *Fides et Ratio,* at all realistic?

II: Threshold of Hope?

Empty victory

Following the 1991 Gulf War between the American-led allies and Iraq, hopes for the world were never so high. The liberation of Kuwait, the battering of Iraq's infrastructure and almost total destruction of the Iraqi dictator's armoury had come hard on the heels of the *annus mirabilis* of 1989, when the Cold War had finally come to an end with the 'springtime of nations' in Central and Eastern Europe. The war against oppression, it seemed, had in all essentials been won; only a few minor battles, to mop up pockets of resistance, would now be necessary. This was the assumption underlying President Bush's announcement of a 'New World Order'. It was also the thesis of a sensational bestseller, Francis Fukuyama's *The End of History and the Last Man* (Hamish Hamilton, 1992); liberal democracy and the markets, Fukuyama told us, had achieved final victory.

With the benefit of hindsight, the grounds for such a claim seem tenuous. Let us first consider the 'victory' of liberal democracy; we can begin with Russia. In 1993 the financier George Soros made the following statement,

> What used to be the Soviet Union may become a black hole which may eventually swallow up civilisation. The disintegration will continue until eventually the goods and services necessary to maintain civilised existence will cease to be available. The process may take a long time, but it is potentially bottomless.

The immediate occasion for this judgement of Soros was Russia's economic crisis of the spring of 1993, when inflation was running at 2,500%, corruption was clearly endemic and there were widespread food and fuel shortages. Disaster was somehow averted, but only after President Boris Yeltsin, in October of that year, had ordered crack troops into Moscow to enforce the state of emergency he had declared when hardline opponents launched an armed uprising. When, in May 1994, Alexander Solzhenitsyn returned to his homeland, he branded Russia's 'democracy' a sham or worse, urging repentance and moral cleansing.

Nearly five years later, at the end of 1998, the fate of democracy in Russia was once again hanging by a thread, in the face of an equally deep crisis: taxes were uncollected, salaries were unpaid (most notably those for the army), the value of the rouble had again plummeted, half the economy was said to be in the hands of organised crime and people in some areas of the country were dispensing with money altogether and resorting to barter. Yeltsin seemed a spent force, with civil control appearing to be wielded less by government than by a few post-Communist barons of industry or the burgeoning mafias, food was scarce, heavy drinking endemic, crime rife, violent deaths commonplace, the suicide rate (one of the worst in the world) rising and the population falling – by 1300 a day. An earlier verdict on Russia, given by population experts, remained valid, 'A society suffering severe social degradation, where family, social, moral and political norms have broken down'.

By the summer of 1999 the economic situation had stabilised. The rouble was no longer in free-fall, there was some inward investment and devaluation had made Russian industry less uncompetitive in price. Yet the political situation remained highly brittle, few daring to predict a swift end to the nation's troubles. The absence of effective government had even led to some far-flung Russian communities becoming virtually self-governing.

To the Western onlooker, who a few years ago witnessed the break-up of the Soviet Union, the possibility of yet further disintegration – that of Russia itself – inevitably suggests itself. The other possibility is reversion to a dictatorial, centralised form of government, running a command economy. But if the latter transpires, the democratic experiment in Russia will have failed.

The prospects for democracy in Eastern Europe apart from Russia seem on the face of it fairly promising, despite the fact that several of these countries are now in the hands of former Communists and one or two, like Romania, in deep social distress. (Former Yugoslavia is a special case; see Chapter III.) These have largely embraced market economics, though they are for the most part cautious, believing in gradual change. The main and very real threat to the fragile flower of democracy in this region is posed by the possibility of a popular backlash following world recession. If people become impatient when they see little tangible fruit from their hard-fought battle and privations suffered in the interests of economic freedom, they are likely to revert to more autocratic models of government.

What of Western Europe?

A few years ago Conor Cruise O'Brien wrote the following (*The Independent*, 2 April 1993),

> Europhiliac insensibility to the feelings and attitudes of national electorates . . . is dangerously widespread in the European political class. . . . The Europhilia of elites, a sentiment not shared by peoples, is doing serious damage to the most vital element in democratic continuity. By this, I mean, quite simply, the

democratic habit. As a habit, an aspect – which only people who never think about history would ignore or despise – democracy flows in national channels, not European ones. To fail to take adequate account of national 'moods' is to try to 'build Europe' on insecure foundations. We should not take democracy for granted, as the Europhiliacs habitually do. Democracy in Europe is under greater threat than at any time since the end of the Second World War.

Writing in the context of the signing of the Maastricht Treaty by John Major's Conservative administration, after Parliament had ratified it by the narrowest of margins, Noel Malcolm pointed out how British democracy was being eroded by European-style government (*The Daily Telegraph,* 30 March 1995),

As more and more areas of British policy-making are assigned to European bodies, our own government ministers find themselves operating increasingly as quasi-diplomats, deciding matters of policy through whatever fixes and fudges they can obtain in the EU Council of Ministers. And the methods of deception and mendacity, which are needed to settle such deals in Brussels, become even more necessary afterwards, at Westminster, where these *faits accomplis* have to be forced through.

Nothing in Europe has changed to make the words of the above two writers any less relevant than they were when written. Indeed, the 'democratic deficit' in European institutions is a constant refrain among Europhiliacs and Eurosceptics alike.

Over the last few years a feature of the scene in the older democracies has been public disenchantment with both political institutions and leaders. In Canada, the Conservative government under Kim Campbell suffered the worst defeat of any governing party in democratic history in 1993, retaining only three parliamentary seats. In Britain, John Major's government achieved unprecedented levels of unpopularity, despite presiding over a flourishing economy, and were finally swept from power in May 1997 in a devastating electoral defeat at the hands of Tony Blair's 'New Labour'; surprisingly but significantly, the turnout of voters for that election fell to 71%, after a 78% turnout in 1992. Italy has still scarcely recovered from the crisis constituted by the fall of Prime Minister Silvio Berlusconi, charged with corruption and links with the Mafia, and finally convicted and given a two year prison sentence. Financial scandals characterised the government of President Mitterrand of France in his final years, with similar charges embarrassing the first administration of his successor, Jacques Chirac, while in Spain Prime Minister Felipe González, accused of corruption and beset by governmental sleaze, earned deep distrust among his electorate.

In Europe as a whole, just 43% of voters turned out for the elections to the European Parliament of 10 June 1999, down from the 63% turnout of twenty years previously. In Britain, the 1999 turnout was a paltry 23 %.

Then there is the USA, where fewer than 50% of eligible citizens bothered to vote in the presidential election of November 1996, which returned Bill Clinton to power for a second term of office. Opinion polls at the time suggested that half those who did vote doubted the President's trustworthiness – with good reason, it turned out, as details of the sex scandal began to emerge. The main result of the latter, as of the subsequent impeachment trial, has probably been the further disillusioning of people with the whole process of politics – a trend which Clinton's eventual acquittal will hardly have halted. The turnout of only 35% of voters in the November 1998 Congressional elections was at the lowest levels since the Second World War.

Finally we have Japan, where the humbling in 1993 of the entire leadership cadre through the uncovering of widespread corruption polluted that country's political atmosphere, and is still producing fall-out. According to polls conducted in 1998, the large majority no longer have faith in either their political institutions or their politicians, and in the wake of the country's economic crisis suicide figures are worse than in the black years of 1945-47. It is scarcely surprising in this climate that a far-right author has been elected governor of Tokyo, one promising wartime-style 'moral education' in schools and blaming the Asian financial crisis on an American plot hatched by a 'Jewish Trio' (Madeleine Albright, Robert Rubin and George Soros). (*The Guardian Weekly*, 18 April 1999).

Democracy may not yet be a casualty in Western Europe, America and Japan, but its condition can scarcely be considered healthy. With regard to the West, Joseph Nye comments, 'The pattern of declining respect for once accepted authority is seen across the western world.' Negative political campaigning, he continues, has further reinforced 'a distaste for and distrust of politicians and government'. (*The Times Higher Education Supplement*, 23 January 1998; see also *Why People Don't Trust Government*, Joseph F. Nye Jr, Philip D. Zelikow and David C. King, eds, Harvard University Press, 1997).

Looking further afield, beyond the older democratic states, the prospects for democracy are hardly rosy.

The African continent, where hopes were so high in the 1950s and 1960s, offers virtually no example of genuine democracy other than that of South Africa. And even there, in the 'rainbow nation', a deeply ingrained pessimism about the future prevails. The reasons are clear: unemployment stands at 33%, the level of violence and crime in the cities is horrific yet still rising (over 60 murders a day and the world's highest incidence of rape), the value of the rand has plunged and, last but not least, the dragon of racism resolutely refuses to die. On top of all this, the rock-like Nelson Mandela has handed over the presidency to a successor.

Such is the situation in Africa's showpiece. Yet for all that, South Africa appears a haven of democratic stability compared to most nations on the continent. In early 1999 there were a dozen armed conflicts in progress in Africa, ranging from small local skirmishes to full-scale warfare, with 120,000 children serving as soldiers according to a report by children's rights groups. As to government, the few pockets of hope today (like Nigeria) only heighten awareness of how unstable and/or oppressive are the majority of regimes. It is true that in recent years there have been plenty of elections. For instance, between 1990 and 1995 no less than 17 out of the 18 African members of the Commonwealth (the countries of once-British Africa, plus Mozambique) held elections; yet in all but two of these, Malawi and Zambia, the old dictators and party bosses, with varying degrees of fiddling and bullying, kept their hold on power. As *The Economist* concluded ('Democracy in Africa', 1 March 1997), 'Elections there may be, but democracy has not yet taken root.'

The Middle East offers Israel as a democracy of sorts. The nations surrounding her (not excluding Turkey) are none of them democracies in the Western sense. But we have already looked at this volatile region in the previous chapter.

Further east, Pakistan 'teeters on the edge of chaos', as *Le Monde* put it in late 1998, or as an observer remarked in February 1999, 'You have to understand that Pakistan no longer has an administration, but it does have a bomb.' Neighbouring India just maintains democratic government, despite popular weariness with politics and politicians, as evinced in April 1999 when a third general election in as many years was announced, and notwithstanding the swelling tide of religiously motivated violence, which surged with particular strength following the Hindu Bharatiya Janata Party's rise to national power in early 1998. The main concern about these two countries centres on the fact that they have both joined the 'nuclear club' at a time when their mutual differences remain unresolved.

China, also a nuclear power and still under Communist rule, seems more interested in liberating the economy than its people; as 1999 progressed fears grew for the stability of the country, faced with mounting unemployment, falling exports, bad debts coming home to roost and a wave of corruption. Meanwhile, North Korea and Burma remain strangers to democracy in any form, Cambodia has 'phoney' elections and Malaysia's 'democratically elected' government is accused of corruption. The fall of the dictator Suharto in Indonesia in June 1998 led to the first steps towards liberalising political activity under his successor Bacharuddin Habibie, including the promise of elections. Violent riots in late 1998 led Habibie to warn protesting students that 'the transition to democracy will take time', yet the elections took place on schedule in June 1999. Whether, as events in East Timor show, a genuine form of democracy will materialise, however, is not assured.

The states of Latin America may largely have swung the way of democracy but they remain areas of violence and unrest, the traffic in drugs and accompanying corruption unabated, particularly in Colombia, Mexico, Peru, Honduras and Brazil. Their economies tend to be at the mercy of every major downturn in world markets.

And so, having considered the alleged victory of democracy at this juncture in history, let us turn to that of the markets.

The markets certainly seem to have won – if by 'won' we understand deregulation and the almost universal attempt by regimes around the world, democratic or otherwise, to submit their economies to the rigours of competition, with 'privatisation' the battle cry. The economic collapse of virtually every socialist state left them little option. But the establishment of a permanently vigorous and stable world economy is something else.

We have already cited George Soros, speaking on Russia in 1993. Let us do so again. Speaking to the US Congress on 15 September 1998, he declared, 'The global capitalist system is coming apart at the seams.' The occasion for this apocalyptic assertion was another financial crisis in Russia. Soros described it as 'a complete meltdown . . . frightening'.

The Russian debacle of late 1998, coming in the wake of the economic depression in East Asia, alarmed others besides George Soros. The British financial commentator Will Hutton described the situation as 'plainly the most serious threat to the world economy since the Second World War' (*The Observer,* 30 August 1998), while President Clinton called for an economic summit of heads of government to address 'the biggest challenge in half a century'. Others likened the scene to that of the 1930s (see Chapter III, below).

Will Hutton's more detailed analysis was sombre. He wrote of 'the risk of a world economic catastrophe . . . growing by the day'. He warned,

> The importance of events in Russia is that they are taking the world financial system yet closer to the edge, and the system is now so structured that losses in one country are transmitted to another with the movements in financial prices vastly exaggerated by the speculative derivative markets. . . . The key to economic stability has always been to tightly regulate banks and finance into conservative and cautious behaviour, and so head off the

tendency embedded in financial markets to overlend, overbuy and rush into cash. The great policy mistake of the 1980s and 1990s has been to neglect this truth and trust in the markets' judgements. We are now about to reap the whirlwind.

A world summit, such as President Clinton called for, might have appeared to answer Hutton's chief complaint that 'political impotence' had accompanied the 'deepening global economic malaise'. However, he went further, arguing how deep-rooted such impotence was,

> Part of the problem is that the principal political actors are so obviously damaged goods – but their weakness reveals a more fundamental problem. We live in an era in which government and political leadership is denigrated and criticised. This is the epoch of the market, of individualism, of globalisation, and of Darwinian belief in economic natural selection. The financial markets have achieved their awesome power because governments have been told and become convinced that the state should not have it. The private sector should become our new governors.

In this context, a further pronouncement of Soros' is relevant. 'I now fear,' he wrote in *Atlantic Monthly* (cited in *Time*, 3 February 1997), 'that untrammelled intensification of laissez-faire capitalism and the spread of market values into all areas of life is endangering our open and democratic society.'

We have come full circle. The markets *have* been victorious – with two corollaries: firstly, the destruction of political power as vested particularly in the nation-state; secondly, self-destruction, that is, destruction of the very financial system that these markets themselves have created. There would seem to be one possible solution to the resultant chaos: a new, global totalitarianism.

Such a future scenario, of a global totalitarianism, would seem to arise from the need to cope with other disturbing features of the international scene. Nuclear proliferation is one such; another is the increased movements of peoples under the general pressure of global overpopulation, but specifically induced by environmental factors, social oppression and ethnic conflict; related to the latter trend is the explosion of urban populations in developing countries (such populations set to double by 2020), this placing even greater strain on cities already disintegrating through the scarcity or prohibitive cost of resources; there is also the increased incidence, since the end of the Cold War, of brush-fire wars and terrorism, as well as the rise of rogue dictators and regimes; finally, there is the relative weakness of existing political institutions, not least the United Nations.

Social morass

Whatever precise form future government takes it is likely in the end to be global because we live today in a society that is global at other levels. As we have seen, we now have a global economy, made possible because we have a global communications system. The latter has been in place to a greater or lesser extent for at least a hundred years. Over the last decade or so, however, it has been refined to a degree hitherto unimagined, the most obvious example of this being the Internet – that global linking of computers by telephone along which vast amounts of information, including sound and moving pictures, can be transmitted instantly.

A conference, *The Governance of Cyberspace*, was held at the Teesside University in April 1995 to examine the legal issues raised by the fast-growing network. One speaker, Dr Roger Burrows, summarised the matter

> The Internet is . . . a network without frontiers, without laws and ,with no one there to say that you cannot say that or you must not see this. Suddenly, governments are waking up to the realisation that this is an information highway without any way to police its users.

Mark Whine, of the Board of Deputies of British Jews, warned the conference that the Internet represented a 'previously undreamed of possibility for both propagating racism and allowing racists to access each other's ideas and resources'. The ghastly potential of the Internet in this direction became apparent when it was learned that the two Nazi-obsessed teenagers responsible for the Denver school massacre of 20 April 1999 (anniversary of Hitler's birthday) in Colorado, USA, had fed their violent fantasies via the Internet. Today's more sophisticated neo-Nazis communicate through an encryption system (developed by an American Nazi-sympathiser) known as PGP ('Pretty Good Privacy'), the individual codes of which are very hard to crack.

The dissemination of pornography is a further unsavoury use to which the Internet is being put. A Newcastle conference of the British Association for the Advancement of Science was told by Professor Harold Thimbleby in September 1995 that the Internet was in reality a heavily used red-light district, piping pornography into millions of homes around the world. His survey of a commonly utilised 'research engine' had shown that half of all searches are aimed at locating pornography. In November 1995 an Interpol conference on crime against children held in London was told that international paedophile rings and child pornographers were making contact on the network using the PGP programme.

Most dramatic was what Dr Stephen Mooney, of the London School of Economics, told the Teesside University conference; he predicted that the development of information technology threatened to undermine the 'foundation, power and authority' of the nation-state, which would suffer fragmentation as economic power was transferred to the 'cyberstate'.

The problems of monitoring and policing superhighways like the Internet has greatly increased the incidence and scope of crime in today's world. The opportunities offered the criminal by the Internet, or indeed by computerization in general, for electronic fraud, industrial espionage, blackmail, the promotion of racism or terrorism and other illicit activities, combined with the problems of detection, have utterly eclipsed previous forms of criminal conduct. The practice of hacking alone has opened the way for the malicious, vindictive or plain crazed to cause mayhem and destruction simply for the sake of it. It is worth recalling that construction details of the bomb that destroyed the federal building in Oklahoma City, USA, on 19 April 1995, when 168 people lost their lives, were published on computer networks; chemicals and fertilisers needed for construction were readily obtainable from petrol stations and garden centres.

Terrorism is the most deadly form of crime, as the American nation was reminded on that Wednesday in 1995, the more deeply as it began to emerge that the worst act of terrorist crime in American history had been home grown. Yet despite the considerable efforts of Western governments, especially those of the USA, this lethal form of activity, far from abating, seems to be on the increase. In December 1995, John Deutch, head of CIA, gave the following warning to the US House of Representatives Intelligence Committee, 'I regret that I have come to the conclusion there is going to be tremendous growth in terrorism over the next decade or so, not only directed towards Americans but throughout the world.' His words have to date been amply fulfilled, the bombings of the American Embassies in Kenya and Tanzania in August 1998, when at least 263 people were killed, being just two among many examples.

In his article already cited in Chapter I (*The Times Higher Education Supplement*, 14 November 1997), the Cambridge historian Christopher Andrew shows how terrorist activity is taking new and disturbing directions. He writes

> The use of sarin on the Tokyo underground in 1995 by the Japanese cult, Aum Shinrikyo, may have been the first example of terrorist use of weapons of mass destruction, but it will not be the last. . . .
> Today's religious and cult-based terrorists are much more menacing than their predecessors. The most dangerous delude themselves into believing that they are doing the will of God in destroying the forces of Satan. . . . Thirty years ago there was not a single religious or cult-based terrorist group anywhere. As recently as 1980 only two of the world's 64 known terrorist groups

were religious. Since then, however, Shi'a extremists alone have probably been responsible for more than a quarter of deaths from terrorism. . . . Terrorists deranged enough to believe that they are doing the will of God are also liable to believe they have divine authority to massacre as many victims as they wish.

Corruption represents a type of crime rather different from that of terrorism, yet its effects are in some ways as deadly. The exposure of such crimes worldwide at a high, frequently governmental level, has soared in recent years. A secretariat of the UN's Ninth Congress on Crime, held in Cairo in April/May 1995, broke a long-standing taboo by issuing a sliding scale of bribery rates for corrupt government officials and world leaders. According to this, some heads of state can be bought for as little as $5 million; corrupt civil servants, politicians and presidents, fall into four categories, with each grade costing about ten times as much to bribe as the one below.

This new 'culture of corruption' was remarkably illustrated early in 1999. In the same week in January the executive leaders of the greatest world powers were being charged with corrupt practice: in Washington, the impeachment trial of President Clinton by the US Senate was getting under way; in Moscow, the Russian Parliament, or Duma, was considering five articles of impeachment against President Yeltsin; in Strasbourg, the European Parliament was voting on whether to dismiss *all twenty* European Union Commissioners for 'fraud, nepotism and mismanagement' (in March they resigned en bloc, with their president, in the face of a damning independent report). Nor was this all. A few days later news broke that members of the International Olympic Committee had received large sums of money, gifts, or sexual favours in return for their support of the bid by Salt Lake City for the Winter Olympics in 2002; six members were subsequently expelled and four resigned. Large-scale corruption might have accompanied other bids, it also emerged.

Wherever one looks today – the Americas, Europe, Africa, Asia, China, the Middle and Far East – it is the same story of corruption, people high or low grabbing what they can get, cheating on their governments, populaces, employers, employees, competitors, clients, wives, the only crime the folly of being caught, and swift denial of 'real' wrongdoing if that happens. It is unnecessary to cite the appalling statistics; 'sleaze' of every description stares up at us from almost every page of news. 'Brazen leaders of the shameless society' was the title of a recent article on the British and world scene (Melanie Phillips, *The Sunday Times*, 27 December 1998).

Crime in general has been rising inexorably for decades. In Britain the annual rate of increase has averaged 5% since the First World War, a figure which the above Congress on Crime estimated as the rate of increase worldwide. The Congress reported that the big syndicates had become mighty corporate empires, with combined turnover exceeding $830 billion. They had developed their trade in services, branching out from the white slave trade to child trafficking and illegal immigration rings which 'served' around a million migrants a year. There was increasing evidence of international alliances and deals between criminal gangs, who had been quick to see the advantages of global economic integration. At a time when countries were easing border restrictions and 'hot' money was moving between countries at the speed of an electronic signal, the rise in international crime was particularly worrying, experts said, especially as money laundering, generating vast amounts of cash, could influence national economies.

The incidence of crime among young people is a particularly worrying statistic. In Britain, juvenile crime has exploded, according to a 1996 government report; this revealed that one in three males under the age of thirty have at some time been convicted of a criminal offence. In the West as a whole juvenile murderers are becoming increasingly common, especially in the USA, where murders by teenagers have tripled in recent years.

Another alarming statistic relates not to murders *by* children but *of* children. According to the U.S. Center for Disease Control, murder rates of American children tripled (and suicide rates quadrupled) between 1950 and the present day (see *The Times*, 8 February 1997). Murder is now the third leading cause of death among US children aged five to fourteen.

Crime, however, is a symptom of something deeper. As well as reflecting an innate anti-social tendency within humanity, it bespeaks a general deterioration in moral standards and resultant loss of social stability – particularly as expressed in the collapse of the family. In Britain, 50% of all pregnancies now occur outside marriage (the proportion reaching nearly 70% in some inner-city areas), over 30% of children are born outside marriage, nearly 25% of all families with dependent children are headed by a single parent and 40% of marriages end in divorce; alongside this, research has established that children from broken homes run greater risks of education, health and behaviour problems. (Office of National Statistics, March 1999; Office of Population Report, 1996; Rowntree Report, 1995). In the European Union as a whole, one in three marriages now break up, the figures having risen sharply over the last thirty years, and in the USA half of all marriages end in failure.

One reason for the breakdown of the family is the changing roles of – not to say conflict between – the sexes. 'Gender' is currently a key concept in academic circles, with departments of 'gender' and women's studies proliferating. Such developments may be worthwhile, yet they also illustrate the confusion in people's minds about sexual qualities, relationships and roles. Writing in *The Washington Post* (14 May 1995) of macho militiamen like Timothy McVeigh, convicted of responsibility for the Oklahoma bombing, Thomas Edsell has shown how significant the changes are,

> In these past three decades, the balance of power between men and women, in the workplace, at home and in bed, has been irrevocably altered. The social consequences of this shift are enormous – immeasurably so in the case of individuals.

Confusion of roles is not confined to 'gender', however. It is the crucial issue underlying the conflict between the generations. For today the authority of parents ('the old') over children, and even more that of teachers (again, 'the old') over their pupils is being challenged. The 'class struggle' is also fuelled by a confusion of roles. 'Egalitarianism' has fostered the notion that in the end no one has a right to exercise authority over another. (Socialist states have dealt with practical problems by declaring that no one is exercising authority since 'the people' are in control!)

In April 1995 the National Association of Schoolmasters and Union of Women Teachers in Britain launched a campaign to protect teachers from the growing threats of attacks by pupils, of which 16,000 were being reported annually. The campaign drew attention to Britain's 'blackboard jungle', similar to that of the USA, where school boards countrywide have had to enact discipline codes requiring year-long expulsion of students threatening violence or caught with a weapon. There were 14,000 expulsions (or 'exclusions') in Britain in 1995, five times as many as in 1990.

Conflict between the sexes, between age groups and age-related authority structures, and between classes – strata in society based on birth or wealth – grievously undermines social stability, yet racial or ethnic conflict is even more destructive. Often masquerading as nationalism, racism has given us a grim new term: 'ethnic cleansing'.

Ethnic crimes have been occurring all round the world over the last decade – in former Yugoslavia, Iraq, Rwanda, the Democratic Republic of Congo (former Zaire), in Somalia, Sudan and all over West Africa, in India, Sri Lanka and Indonesia – to name only the most prominent examples. Something near to 'ethnic cleansing' occurred at the hands of the Russians in Chechnya in the mid-1990s, and, with popular concern about the immigrant 'threat' and racist and anti-semitic attacks by right-wing extremists increasing in Germany by nearly a third in 1997, even Western Europe is haunted – once again – by the spectre of ethnic killing.

With this in mind, German intelligence services are concerned about the Internet's unpoliceable 'Thule Net', tending to 'the intellectualisation of the Right'. Germany's National Security chief had this to say following an arson attack on a hostel for asylum-seeking refugees in Lübeck in January 1996 (*The Daily Telegraph*, 21 January 1996) ,

> A right-wing intellectual-led movement like that of 1968 will have a far greater effect on society than the Left ever achieved. . . . The Right has gone underground and reorganised itself, keeping a lower profile and modelling itself on the anarchist Red Army Faction terrorist cells that emerged from the 1968 student riots.

He pointed to the fiftieth anniversaries marking the end of the Second World War as the moment at which the Right gained new respectability and spoke of the attention given since then by students and young intellectuals to right-wing historians and politicians with unorthodox interpretations of the War.

In Britain, racial attacks and intimidation, and racially related crime, are rising at the rate of 8% annually, and Scotland Yard has become so worried by the proliferation of underground neo-Nazi groups that it has formed a special unit to tackle the problem. In April 1999 three bomb attacks in London, for which hard-right groups claimed responsibility, raised fears of a new, escalating wave of racist violence. Such trends are deeply disturbing, yet they have not so far translated into success in elections for racist parties; the same cannot be said of Europe as a whole, however.

The dramatic progress of far-right political parties with racist agendas in continental Europe can be charted (*cf.* Lee, Martin, *The Beast Reawakens*, Little, Brown, 1997).

In 1984 the French National Front won 11% in the European elections. Commentators brushed this aside as an aberration, but within a few years the pattern was being repeated elsewhere. In 1989 Jorg Haider, leader of the Austrian hard-right Freedom Party, was elected governor of the southern province of Carinthia. (In March 1999 his party was outright winner there, with 42% of the vote, and the following month he was re-elected governor, eight years after being forced to resign for praising Hitler's labour policies). In 1993 the largest party in Antwerp, Belgium, was a Fascist party, the Vaams Blok. By 1994, Italy had Fascists in the cabinet, and Gianfranco Fini, neo-Fascist leader of the country's National Alliance, was describing Hitler's ally Mussolini as 'the greatest statesman of the twentieth century'. By 1998, far-right parties had gained over 20% of the vote in parliamentary elections in Austria, 15% or more in Italy and France, 10% in Belgium and Denmark, and over 5% in the Czech Republic. In other countries, like Germany, such parties had made erratic but spectacular appearances at a regional level. Gary Younge has summed the matter up (*The Guardian Weekly*, 28 June 1998), 'As we approach the twenty-first century, Fascism has reinvented itself as a mainstream ideology in European politics.'

The happiness thing

The relentless rise in crime, whatever form it takes, is scarcely more harmful to social cohesion than the modern obsession with personal happiness.

The pursuit of happiness is today considered an 'inalienable right'. This is thanks chiefly to Thomas Jefferson, who included it, together with 'life and liberty' in his draft for the American Declaration of Independence of 1776. Since then, this 'right' has been assiduously pursued by all who enjoy any freedom to choose the way they live. And 'happiness', we are assured today, is supremely sexual fulfilment.

We see this on every side in Britain. Fashion shows have titles like *Erotic Zones*, the costumes featuring semi-nudity. On TV chat shows people achieve instant fame by intimate sexual disclosures, while comedians assail us with erotic talk and symbolism – both 'straight' and 'gay'. Nudity and explicit love-making are virtually *de rigueur* in films, and increasingly common in the theatre. Naked actors and actresses go on show in London art galleries. Many newspapers and magazines, and most new novels, are semi-pornographic by the standards of yesterday. As for specialist videos, no sexual territory is left to conquer.

Cataloguing the evidence is scarcely necessary, for almost anywhere you go in the world today you can be confident there will be reminders – especially through advertising, in the media and on hoardings – of the importance of being sexually active. Huge sums are spent on the sex trade, London's being worth $310 million annually, 30% more than London Transport's annual turnover, according to a 1997 survey by Middlesex University.

Sexual gratification has indeed become a near-synonym for happiness. Yet to what end? It is salutary to recall that the Romans of the late Empire period, sated with orgies and shameless hedonism, lacked the will to defend themselves against the Barbarians, and so lost their Empire – just as late eighteenth-century French society, and the German Weimar Republic of the early twentieth century, both notorious for looseness of morals and the blatant sexuality of their art forms, were overwhelmed by a different but no less terrible fate.

Having done their best to trap happiness for themselves, modern people seek to ensure that no one takes it from them. So they are meticulous about security, protecting themselves and their families, their homes, their cars, and other possessions, with elaborate locks and alarms. Not content with this, they take out expensive insurance policies against the loss of, or hurt to, every conceivable object or person of value in their lives. The importance of obvious safety precautions is not in dispute; today, however, safety and the 'protection' offered by insurance is considered next to godliness.

Such is the case with personal insurance; corporate insurance is much bigger business. The crisis that a few years ago hit Lloyd's of London, the world's oldest and best known insurance market, gives some indication of what is involved, and the vulnerable nature of the whole enterprise. Facing claims amounting to billions of dollars, following unprecedented disasters occurring several years in succession, the whole market at one point seemed likely to collapse, individual 'Names', or underwriters, being unable or unwilling to pay up. Only a year or two later, when the scale of claims had subsided and the 'Names' had accepted modified liability (their dues subsidised), was the market in the clear.

The Lloyd's affair also focused attention on litigation – a feature of life today that has, as no other, upset the equilibrium in the world of insurance. The immense increase in the number of lawsuits affects not only underwriters, but also corporations, large and small, as well as individuals such as doctors and architects. These are being forced to pay such crippling premiums that many have decided the whole exercise is pointless, so have simply stopped trading, or working. In May 1999 a woman was suing SwissAir for $1.2 billion for a 1998 plane crash; meanwhile, the US light aircraft industry has virtually gone out of business because of litigation, or litigation fears.

In the USA, indeed, the situation is almost out of control. In the case of childbirth, the odds of the 'midwife' being sued are so high that no baby is delivered without prepayment of at least $1000 insurance premium. Awards for damages, or out of court settlements, defy belief. The K Mart supermarket group paid $10 million to a woman shot and paralysed by her boyfriend because it sold him the rifle; the New York transport authority paid $9 million to a Mexican restaurant worker who got drunk and fell in front of a train, losing an arm; in April 1995 a woman was awarded compensation of $19 million by an American court for the death of her husband in the Lockerbie air disaster. In Britain a similar situation is developing, the 'compensation culture' costing the public sector $2.9 billion annually, according to a 1999 report by the Centre for Policy Studies.

The mania for litigation, which has gripped the USA and is spreading to Britain and further, is another manifestation of our generation's chief obsession. It is just one more way of pursuing the 'right' to happiness.

Happiness, of course, being an abstract, subjective concept, covers every object of man's desire, and therefore includes every kind of 'right'. Life and liberty can be considered aspects of happiness, as can health (or medical care), work, a reasonable standard of living, political self-determination (a form of liberty), and so on. But whatever labels are given to 'inalienable human rights', the fact that people today believe they have them has fostered the angry, grasping sense of grievance so characteristic of our age.

A short cut to happiness for many people today is some form of gambling. In Britain, according to a B.B.C. report of October 1997, nine out of ten adults and two out of three adolescents now gamble, with more and more becoming addicts. Meanwhile, a 1997 study at Manchester Metropolitan University revealed that cries for help to Gamblers Anonymous had risen by 61% since the National Lottery started in 1994, one researcher commenting that the introduction of the Lottery had created a 'gambling free-for-all and a breeding ground for social ills'.

Two examples of such ills can be cited. In April 1995 a Liverpool man, Mr Tim O'Brien, shot himself on discovering that though his regular sequence of numbers for the Lottery appeared to entitle him to a $3.2 million share in the jackpot, he had forgotten to renew his entry; he was married, had two children and was a keen churchgoer. At about the time of Mr O'Brien's death, a man who had the previous December won $28.5 million on the Lottery was being sued by a friend who claimed they had agreed to split any prize money.

Not that lotteries account for more than a small proportion of the total expended on gambling. In casinos around the world, in betting shops, at racecourses and dog circuits, in bingo halls, drinking saloons, coffee-houses, barracks and homes billions of dollars are staked on every twist and turn of 'lady luck' – though seldom to the permanent enrichment of the punter. In the USA, gambling is the fastest growing industry, currently generating $50 billion in annual revenue and causing an estimated 15.4 million Americans to be problem or pathological gamblers (see the report of the National Gambling Impact Study Commission, 1999). The boom has occurred, firstly, because of the lure of the get-rich-quick passport to happiness, and, secondly, because gambling is so deeply addictive. After the death of Mr O'Brien, a Liverpool newsagent explained the problem, 'The Lottery is like a drug. Some can't go for a week without their "fix" of tickets. I'm afraid it is taking over people's lives. It is deadly.'

Addiction to gambling is psychological; to drugs it is chemical – and no less deadly.

The world's drug trade has grown dramatically, according to a UN report of July 1997, accounting for over 8% of international trade, or

$400 billion annually. It is the world's biggest business, after the arms trade, some $80 billion of the total being laundered into the global financial system.

In Britain the drug trade was estimated in July 1998 (Office of National Statistics) to be worth some $16 billion, or 2.5% of all consumer spending. Over six million people in England and Wales use drugs, a 1995 study revealed, and nearly half of Britain's schoolchildren have experimented with an illegal drug by the age of sixteen (House of Commons report, 1996). Heroin and cocaine are believed to lie behind 7% of all crime, while an estimated half of the $6.4 billion property crime is drug related; drug enforcement costs $800 million annually, with MI5 and MI6 involved, 1,300 specialist police officers and 600 Customs drug investigators. Meanwhile, according to unpublished results from a national audit carried out for the government 'Drug Czar', Keith Hellawell, the drive against drugs in Britain is proving ineffective (*The Guardian Weekly*, 28 March 1999). On the social consequences, Paul Goodman has written (*The Sunday Telegraph*, 7 May 1995):

> The drug trade now menaces not simply our economic and social development, but the very stability of our political order and constitutional settlement. . . . Our cities are slowly being transformed, with some districts becoming no-go areas.

In the USA, where profits are around $150 billion and there are 3.6 million addicts, drug abuse is thought to contribute to over half of the 20,000 annual murders. By 1996 it was clear that the federal government's 'war on drugs', declared in 1986, had largely failed – the number of drug users remaining at about 40 million, the consumption of marijuana, sometimes laced with cocaine, increasing among teenagers, heroin making a comeback among people of all ages, and the production of coca in Colombia growing. In 1997 it was reported that drug use had doubled among teenagers over the previous five years. Drugs on the streets in the USA today 'are stronger, cheaper, more pure, and more widely available than at any time in history', writes Mike Gray (*Drug Crazy: How We Got into This Mess and How We Can Get Out*, Random House, 1999), drug smugglers having, according to a State Department report, replaced straightforward trafficking routes with 'a complex web of nodes and lines linking virtually every country in the world to the main drug production and trafficking centres'.

Drug abuse can be seen as an aspect of the 'pursuit of happiness', especially in relation to the young, ready to experiment (sometimes fatally) with any new and pleasurable source of experience; for some in this modern era, however, it can be a response to stress, and depression. In surveys carried out in Britain in 1995, Susan de Vere found that 25% of women suffered from stress and 50% from depression, while for men the figures were 60% in each case. Stress, she said, was 'the disease of the Nineties'.

There are an estimated 330 million people suffering from depression worldwide (though many cases go undiagnosed), $7 billion is spent on anti-depressants (the sum increasing yearly), and by 2020 it will be the second most disabling disease (*The Economist*, 19 December 1998). In Britain, according to a B.B.C. report of April 1999, the incidence of depression had doubled over the previous four or five years and there were nine million patient cases involving the condition annually. Meanwhile, the largest component of the $6.9 billion National Health Service spending on drugs (medicines) is treatments for the nervous system, including anti-depressants, while mental health problems overall cost an estimated $51.2 billion annually (*The Guardian Weekly*, 19 October 1997).

Not surprisingly, in view of all this, many today are looking for some new, all-embracing – even transcendent – answer to life's many questions and problems.

At the end of his book on cosmology, *A Brief History of Time* (Bantam Press, 1988), Stephen Hawking writes, 'If we find the answer . . . it would be the ultimate triumph of human reason – for then we would know the mind of God.' He is referring to the possibility of discovering a complete theory of the universe – the final, total answer to every question about man and his cosmic environment. Having addressed such a task, he has been voted by the reading public number one science guru, his slim volume having become one of the best sellers of all time after the Bible.

Bryan Appleyard has this to say in his own book (*Understanding the Present: Science and the Soul of Modern Man*, Pan, 1992),

> Hawking's tone and his conception of the significance of his work are typical of a certain way of presenting science. . . . God is often evoked. . . . Bringing God into the equation suggests both the importance and the virtue of the scientific enterprise – this, we are being told, is a continuation of the ancient religious quest to find Him and to do His will. The message is that science is *the* human project. It is what we are intended to do. It is the only adventure.

Stephen Hawking's popularity, his elevation to a kind of High Priesthood of his metier, is not the only symptom of science as a quasi-religion. Arthur C. Clarke, doyen of English science fiction writers, believes that there are no limits to what the human race can achieve through science; there are only economic, political and legal bars. The biggest advance of the last 50 years, he says, has been the unravelling of the human genetic code, and over the next 50 years the greatest breakthroughs will come in genetic engineering and genetic-based medicine. Mankind will eventually develop techniques for living much longer – or for ever. This will give time, among other things, for man to colonise the galaxies, or the latter will be achieved by cheating the speed of light and slipping through other dimensions to get from A to B.

Clarke is probably right about the last 50 years, and perhaps about the next. The study of the molecule DNA submitted to the journal *Nature* on 2 April 1953 by James Watson and Francis Crick has been called the most important scientific paper published in the twentieth century. But slipping through other dimensions? Living for ever – as physical beings? This is not even religion; it is superstition.

Religion in the traditional sense – the world religions like Judaism, Christianity (as usually understood), Islam, Buddhism, Hinduism, as well as the newer religious cults – has also become a focus of superstition. Wonders abound in our age if we are to believe the initiated: madonnas weeping blood, statues drinking milk, every nuance of charismatic blessing, healings, visions, prophecies, revelations. Miracle-a-page books are on every bookstall, in synagogue, church, mosque, temple. Advertisements in newspapers tell of supernaturally inspired preachers possessing the secret of perfect health, spiritual power, global peace.

Many such figures, of course, are associated with one or other of the cults. These are very varied. At one end of the spectrum we have the military-style Aum Shinrikyo cult (one of an estimated 180,000 in Japan), with its 10,000 members formed into a strict hierarchy of 13 different uniformed levels, its spartan conditions for the 'lower ranks', and cruel punishments for those who err. Formed in 1987 to prepare for and preach 'Armageddon in 1997', its leader, Shoko Asshara, a professed admirer of Hitler, was arrested in May 1995 and charged with perpetrating the Tokyo gas attack. In the middle of the spectrum we might place the Church of the Latter Day saints, or Mormons. Founded in New York State in 1820 by Joseph Smith, who claimed to have had a vision of God and received an angelic message, the movement has grown steadily. It is very rich, owning most of Utah and parts of Hawaii, plus land elsewhere and various business concerns; some hardline members are said still to practise polygamy. At the opposite end of the spectrum from Aum Shinrikyo must be Transcendental Meditation, founded in 1958 by Maharashi Yogi. Taken up briefly by the Beatles in the 1960s, its followers believe that collective meditation can solve the world's problems. Other notable cults are Jehovah's Witnesses, Christian Science, New Thought, Unity, Children of God, the Unification Church, Hare Krishnas, Scientology, Rosicrucianism, Yoga, Rajneesh Ashram and the Divine Light Mission.

There is, finally, the New Age movement. Essentially a collection of cults, incorporating mystical, holistic, spiritualistic and vaguely occult beliefs, it represents a rapidly expanding religious trend. It is in reality far from new, its name indicating the foundation on which it is built: astrology. The movement in fact heralds a new era supposed to be dawning in the universe, the Age of Aquarius – one of 'humanism, brotherhood and occult happenings'. The overtly occult, like the sex or sacrificial rituals practised by Satanic groups in Italy or Brazil, can hardly be labelled 'New Age', yet the movement's ideas often constitute a stepping stone to such practices.

Astrology is the most significant aspect of the New Age movement, yet health – or, in New Age parlance, 'holistic health' – runs it a close second. Both have an avid following outside New Age circles.

Even 'quality' papers frequently have an astrology section today, while bookshops and newsagents are piled high with magazines (over a hundred titles in the USA alone), books and booklets on the effect the stars have on human life. Many people (former first lady Nancy Reagan allegedly one of them) find it difficult making any decision without first consulting their personal horoscope.

As for health, leaving aside such New Age notions as the healing power of crystals, we have only to consider the immense popularity of 'health foods', the multiplication of health centres, fitness clubs, massage parlours and the like, not to speak of today's obsession with sexual potency, to realise the depth of our infatuation with 'the body beautiful'. The Reebock Sports Club of New York goes even further. According to Kate Muir (*The Times*, 10 May 1995) this vast, cathedral-like supergym 'is ministering to its Upper West Side neighbourhood in the way that churches once did. It is a "total lifestyle concept", providing succour, healing, a lifting of guilt and a sense of community'.

The pursuit of happiness – whatever really 'happiness' means – consumes a vast amount of people's time and energy. Yet there is scant evidence that they find what they are looking for. Rather, it seems, are people today more heavily burdened than ever with problems. So it is that they seek an answer in superstition, which may find its focus in science, the older religions, one or other of the cults, or in such New Age fads as astrology or bodily health.

Happiness, of course, is a purely human concern, primarily that of individuals; *health* has wider connotations.

Sick planet?

'The only significant factor that coincides with the deterioration of the planet's health over the last century is the dramatic increase in the world's human population. The key issue for the conservation of our natural environment is to find ways of protecting it from the consequences of the human population explosion. We are stretching the Earth's systems like a small child blowing up a balloon. If it goes on blowing, the crucial question is, when is it going to burst?'

The words are those of the Duke of Edinburgh at Windsor Castle on 30 April 1995, speaking in his capacity as International President of the World Wide Fund for Nature. He was addressing a world summit on religion and conservation, called at his own suggestion. Commentators described his words as 'an apocalyptic warning'.

It took the whole of human history until the early nineteenth century for the world population to reach one billion. (It was an estimated 200 million at the time of Christ.) We had reached two billion at the end of the 1920s. The third arrived in 1960, the fourth in 1976, the fifth in 1987. There are now about six billion people on the planet, with some 78 million being added each year. Though the rate of increase is tending slowly to drop, there is little doubt that – barring a worldwide catastrophe – during the twenty-first century two or three billion more people will be crowding onto the earth's surface. Mr Ismail Serageldin, a World Bank vice-president and development expert from Egypt, summed up the situation as he saw it in 1995, 'Whether we stabilise the population at 8.5 billion rather than 10 or 12 billion in the next century, the pressures are coming.'

In September 1997, James Wolfensohn, president of the World Bank, warned the prosperous nations against ignoring the gap between rich and poor,

> We must recognise that we are living with a time bomb and unless we take action now, it could explode in our children's faces. If we do not act, in 30 years the inequities will be greater. With population growing at 80 million a year, instead of three billion living on under $2 a day, it could be as high as five billion.

The independent Worldwatch Institute, based in Washington DC, has focused on diminishing resources, 'Evidence that the world is on an economic path that is environmentally unsustainable can be seen in shrinking fish catches, falling water tables, declining bird populations, record heat waves and dwindling grain stocks.' Dr Lester Brown, Director of the Institute, predicted in February 1996 that high food prices and food scarcity 'could become the defining issue of the new era'.

The 'food crisis' is, of course, not the only problem facing mankind as a result of the population explosion. The greatly increased movements of peoples is another, as we have seen. A more terrible one is 'ethnic cleansing'. Rwanda is the most densely populated country in Africa, and it has been argued that overcrowding was a factor in the 1994 tragedy, when some 800,000 Rwandans were massacred. Once the pressure becomes too great, men will sometimes act like animals, fighting desperately for territory, which spells life's essentials of shelter, food, and above all water.

In September 1998 a spokesman for the Population Association, USA, told the B.B.C. that by 2025 an estimated three billion people would have no access to clean water, and UN water experts meeting in Geneva in February 1999 warned that by 2050 more than two billion would be facing severe shortages. (See also Gleick, P. H., *The World's Water: The Biennial Report on Freshwater Resources 1998-1999*, Island Press, 1999.) Mr Serageldin has said bluntly, 'The wars of the next century will be over water.'

The danger of future conflict arising over water was raised by the French president, Jacques Chirac, in March 1998. Emphasising that water consumption was doubling every twenty years, he proposed an International Academy for Water, to be under the UN Environment Programme, which could supervise the setting up of reliable water networks around the world. The cost, he said, would be $400 billion, but all would contribute. Yet this far-sighted scheme has been still-born, the USA opposing it on the grounds that poorer countries believe water should be free.

Water has already been a precipitating factor in at least one war. In their book *Water Wars: Coming Conflicts in the Middle East* (Gollancz, 1993), John Bulloch and Adel Darwish cite words of Ariel Sharon, the former Israeli general, 'People generally regard 5 June 1967 as the day the Six Day War began. This is the official date. But, in reality, it started two-and-a-half years earlier, on the day Israel decided to act against the diversion of the Jordan.'

The Jordan represents one important Middle East river system; the other two are the Nile and the Tigris-Euphrates. The Nile causes tension between Egypt, wholly dependent on it for water, and the countries upstream: Sudan; Ethiopia, where the Blue Nile and its tributaries rise; the central African countries, which control the main source of the White Nile. Sudan has already played the 'Nile card' against Egypt, having threatened to withhold Nile waters after being accused of complicity in the attempt on President Mubarak's life in June 1995.

The Tigris and Euphrates rise in Turkey, as does the Euphrates tributary Great Zab. The Tigris briefly touches Syria before flowing into Iraq and thence into the Arabian Gulf. The Euphrates and the Great Zab flow into Syria, where they combine before entering Iraq. In January 1990 Turkey stopped the flow of the Euphrates to fill the vast Ataturk Dam. This caused water shortages in Iraq as well as Syria, at which the two countries immediately drew up concerted plans for armed retaliation, forcing Turkey to bring forward its date for allowing the river to flow again. Despite this setback, Turkey is continuing with its GAP Project to build dams and reservoirs on the Euphrates and Tigris, intending shortly to start work on a $1.5 billion project to build the Ilisu dam on the Tigris, 65 kilometres upstream of the Syrian-Iraq border. In May 1999 Syria protested to Britain for supporting this plan.

The population explosion is not in theory irreversible. International conferences on Population and Development, like that held in Cairo in 1994, have considered plans to curb population growth. The above conference assumed that the women of the world hold the key to the problem, and agreed on steps to educate women and improve access to family planning. However, these steps were opposed by the Vatican, by Roman Catholic Latin American countries, a number of Islamic countries or fundamentalist movements, and feminist lobbies. Glib optimism about controlling population growth through the co-operation of world womanhood is therefore misplaced.

Assuming the world population continues to grow at roughly the current rate during the twenty-first century, are we faced with environmental and social apocalypse? Or even if there is no further significant rise in the population, have we already been so profligate with the world's resources and generally irresponsible that disaster is round the corner?

As regards the environment, there has been little, if any, progress. In October 1997 the World Wide Fund for Nature reported that two thirds of the world's forests had already been lost for ever, and what remained was being cut down and burned at an ever increasing rate, an area the size of England and Wales disappearing each year. Only 2% of the remaining forests were protected, it warned, despite the fact that 10% of each forest needed to be saved to prevent mass destruction of species inhabiting it. The publication of these facts occurred just three months after the June/July 1997 UN Earth Summit Review Conference had 'ended in shambles' (*The Guardian Weekly*, 6 July 1997), there having been no agreement on the goals of new aid for developing countries or protecting forests.

A serious dilemma relates to the question of protecting the forests, however, as a recent report explains (*The Guardian Weekly,* 13 September 1998),

> In the past twelve years, another billion mouths have been added
> to the world's population. Crop yields are not keeping pace. But
> population continues to grow. The world will need at least 200
> million new hectares of cropland in the next 30 years to feed the
> planet. But there are only 93 million hectares available for farms
> to expand into – and most of these are forested.

Deforestation is a primary cause of soil erosion, at calamitous levels worldwide, and it is believed to be a contributory factor in the changing patterns of the world's climate and weather. The reality of global warming, attributed partly to the burning of fossil fuels, seems beyond dispute, the 1990s having seen the five hottest years on record (1998 being the hottest of all), glaciers retreating everywhere and big chunks breaking off the Arctic ice mass. Floods of unprecedented severity have afflicted many parts of the world during the decade, the USA suffering three 'once in a 100 years' floods in successive years, the 'worst floods in a millennium' hitting Central Europe in the summer of 1997, China and Bangladesh enduring the most destructive floods of the century in the summer of 1998, and finally Hurricane Mitch devastating Central America in the fall of 1998, floods and landslides ruining infrastructures, causing 11,000 deaths and creating three million homeless in what has been described as the worst natural disaster in modern history. Meanwhile, the world's most important grain-producing areas are short of water, the Ukraine breadbasket drying out and the great plains of Texas threatening to go the same way.

A spokesman of the UN Environment Programme Insurance Initiative told the B.B.C. in January 1999 that the scale and number of disasters resulting from typhoons, hurricanes or earthquakes, particularly where these had led to flooding, had increased significantly over a period of 30 years, and in June 1999 the International Red Cross announced that 1998 had been the worst year on record for natural disasters, with climate change the chief cause. 'Mega natural disasters' were predicted by the Red Cross for the first decade of the new millennium.

There are other ecological worries. The liberal use of chemicals for agricultural and other purposes is one, not least the damaging effect chemical waste is having on marine life. Another is the need to preserve the world's fish stocks from the scourge of overfishing. A third is the potential risk to human health from genetically modified (GM) food, the British Medical Association calling in May 1999 for a ban on imports of unlabelled GM foods and a moratorium on the commercial planting of GM crops until there was 'a scientific consensus on safety'. Yet another is atmospheric pollution, arising in part from 'greenhouse gases', especially as emitted from motor vehicles. Some big cities, like Los Angeles, Mexico City, Athens, Cairo, Bangkok, Delhi, and at times London, can be hit very badly, toxic fumes reaching dangerous levels. Pollution expert Derek Olson has written (*The Times Higher Education Supplement*, 7 March 1997), 'The health of as many as 1.6 billion people living in urban areas throughout the world may be at risk from poor air quality.'

The resurgence or emergence of human diseases has also caused concern.

In May 1998 the British Government was warned by a science and technology committee that misuse of antibiotics in intensive farming, as well as over-prescribing by doctors, could undo the twentieth century miracle of taming killer diseases such as tuberculosis and meningitis. The committee's report stated, 'There is dire prospect of returning to the pre-antibiotic era.' The report warned that bacteria or 'super bugs', known as MRSA, resistant to antibiotics used as last resort treatments for patients, were now prevalent in hospitals. The bugs had become resistant because similar antibiotics had been used for 20 years on farms to promote the growth of intensively reared chickens, turkeys, pigs, sheep and cows.

The World Health Organisation also warned, in 1998, of the appearance of antibiotic-resistant strains of disease, instancing malaria, meningitis, gonorrhoea, typhoid, pneumonia and tuberculosis. There was, it said, a danger of a global plague of tuberculosis, drug-resistant strains having become common in the worst affected areas, such as Russia. A conference in Copenhagen in September 1998 was told that, if nothing was done, antibiotics would not work in 20 years time, and that drug-resistant bacteria would spread lethal diseases worldwide.

On a slightly different level are fears about the emergence of new infectious diseases, which may or may not be directly attributable to man's misuse of the resources available to him. According to a B.B.C. report of April 1997, as many as 30 new diseases had appeared during the previous 20 years, including Ebola, Hepatitis C, and the HIV virus (AIDS). The last is especially worrying: endemic in the West, it has reached pandemic proportions in parts of Asia and much of Africa (see *The Economist*, 2 January 1999).

In 1997 a bleak headline straddled the front page of *The Guardian Weekly* (2 February). It referred to the environmental crisis, 'World turning blind eye to catastrophe.' As long ago as 1992, Dr Lester Brown, Director of the Worldwatch Institute, had spelt out the radical steps necessary if such catastrophe was to be averted, 'Building an environmentally sustainable future depends on restructuring the global economy. It calls for major shifts in reproductive behaviour and dramatic changes in values and lifestyles.' (*Cf. further*, Brown, L R., M. Renner and C. Flavin; L. Starke, ed.; *Vital Signs 1998-99: The Environmental Trends That Are Shaping Our Future*, Earthscan, 1999.)

Whether one is hopeful about the world's environmental future depends on one's confidence in man's ability – and willingness – to take the steps required. Precedents do not encourage much optimism; neither does a realistic assessment of human nature.

The deepest threat

We have come a long way since the Gulf War of early 1991, when the idea of a 'New World Order' was floated. It has turned out to be a chimera, predicated as it was on the assumption that a reformed Soviet Union would join hands with the Western Alliance to police the world. There was the further assumption, given expression by Francis Fukuyama, that a great victory for worldwide democracy, economic prosperity and peace had been won by the fall of Communism.

Both assumptions were misplaced. Russia, only the core of the old Soviet Union, is in no position to be a global policeman, with or without help; on the contrary, the country now constitutes one of the world's most serious problems. The role of policeman has largely devolved upon the United States of America, the European Union up to now showing itself more or less unable to act in a united manner in matters of foreign policy. There is no other nation besides the USA with the economic or military strength, let alone inclination, to shoulder the responsibility. And even the USA, having burned its fingers more than once, as in Somalia, and notwithstanding its role (through Nato) in the Kosovo crisis, displays mixed feelings about continuing in the role. Indeed, the operation against Yugoslavia shows signs of being so costly and the whole 'Balkan problem' so massive and intractable that it could (like Vietnam) provoke a revulsion of popular opinion in USA against future major deployment of the US military overseas. If this transpires, and if, further, the financial turmoil we have been witnessing leads to global recession like that of the 1930s, we could yet see Washington retreating into pre-war style political isolation and economic protectionism.

In his book *On Future War* (Brassey's, 1991) Martin Van Crefeld substitutes for George Bush's 'New World Order' a world of chaos and cruelty, where fanaticism and terrorism prevail. The Cold War, he argues, was the world's last good time, when superpowers collaborated (whatever their ideological differences) in forcing rogue rulers to come to heel, and cracked down on terrorist movements which did not serve their interests. In the new era, he predicts, state authority will atrophy as power passes from elected governments to the robber barons of drugs, computer banking fraud, religious fanaticism, extreme nationalism, or various forms of political crankiness.

Van Crefeld may be overstating the case; we are left, notwithstanding, with a world that so far from being on the verge of a golden age of peace and prosperity has seldom been so fragmented and unstable. And it is precisely this global fragility, half-consciously perceived, that has moved politicians in Europe, and to some extent elsewhere (South-East Asia, for example, where 500 million people from ten nations enjoy a tariff-free area), to push, sometimes in the teeth of popular feeling, for confederation in some form. As the world fragments along ancient tribal or national fault-lines at the popular level, so leaders feel constrained to glue it together again at the political level. At the micro-level we have disintegration; at the macro-level integration, with each process encouraging the other!

There are many threats to mankind as we enter the new millennium. There could be global war; there could be worsening floods, drought, famine; there could be new pandemics of disease and plague; there could be severer earthquakes, a cosmic collision even. All these are possible. One threat, however, seems certain of fulfilment.

Over eight years after George Bush, on 28 February 1991, ordered an end to military action in Iraq (its army crushed, its capital prostrate, its economy in ruins), we today have the spectacle of Saddam Hussein still in power. His army is in place; his weapons of mass destruction are *not* destroyed; his regime is able to provoke confrontation with the UN and the USA – and have the last word. Who would have believed that the tyrant brought to his knees in 1991 would still be posing a threat?

Yet we know that one of the reasons for President Bush's reluctance to smash Iraq completely and so topple or kill Saddam Hussein (besides the desire not to be, or not to be thought, inhumane) was the conviction that some form of stable government, even the most cruel and oppressive, is better than none. Similar thinking lay behind the UN's withdrawal from Somalia in March 1995, abandoning the country to a likely dictatorship under General Aideed, on whose head $25,000 had been placed in 1993. Dictatorship, it was (and is) recognised, is preferable to chaos.

In the world of today it is chaos which is the deepest threat – chaos releasing the world's armies to destroy, plunder and rape, chaos in the money markets overturning the delicately balanced world economy, chaos ripping apart the social fabric of nations, chaos in the environment, spawning disease and death.

If chaos is the threat, and democracy is not working, where does that leave us?

III: Extending the Trends

We have been looking, in our first two chapters, at the way the world is going on the threshold of a new millennium. We began at 'the centre' and worked outwards – Jerusalem, Israel/Palestine, the Middle East, the world. Of course, there is no scientific justification for following medieval practice and placing a relatively small Levantine city at the very hub of history. Yet, as we have seen, Jerusalem has over the last three millennia or so been involved in some of the world's most crucial, seminal events; it has, at the very least, been a major world crossroads.

So what has emerged from our survey? Or, to return to the question posed at the end of the Chapter I, are Pope John Paul's hopes for 'a new world, a new Europe, and a new civilisation' realistic? Put differently, is human thought and endeavour moving broadly in the right direction, as he appears to believe?

In the light of the trends we have identified, an affirmative answer seems impossible. As a reviewer wrote of the Pontiff's book at the time of publication (Damien Thompson, *The Daily Telegraph*, 20 October 1994), 'It is likely to surprise observers with its optimism.' John Paul, it is true, qualifies his high hopes by his choice of quotation from André Malraux, 'The twenty-first century will be the century of religion or it will not be at all.' He thus allows that the world could soon see catastrophe if there is not some sort of revival of 'religion'. However, the implication is, firstly, that such a revival will occur, and, secondly, that it will be beneficial. We may in fact conjecture, on the basis of Dr Navarro-Valls' assurance to us that the book is 'not a testament but a programme', that John Paul sees himself or his successor at the Vatican playing a central role in such a revival. Many, however, will be disposed to query the second assumption that 'religion' is beneficial. The point is debatable, as we have seen; a 'century of religion' could be the worst possible news for mankind.

The fact is, religion *has* revived in the closing years of the second millennium, which very revival has fuelled a particularly disturbing trend. We have referred to this trend already; let us now take a closer look, then turn our attention to a second trend, equally ominous in its way.

Ethnic conflict, financial turmoil

If anything is clear today, it is that ethnic conflict – the bitter fruit of tribalism, nationalism, racism – is on the increase. What is often overlooked, however, is the fact that the emotions and tensions underlying this trend are nourished by religious differences. Indeed, it is frequently religion that best defines the 'ethnicity' over which violence or conflict occurs. This is essentially the case in the Arab/Israeli confrontation; it is most vividly apparent, however, in the strife afflicting the Balkans or former Yugoslavia. The latter provides an instructive example of this whole phenomenon.

A book highlighting the religious dimension to Serb aggression and 'ethnic cleansing' in the Balkans is Michael A. Sells' *The Bridge Betrayed: Religion and Genocide in Bosnia* (University of California Press, 1996). Sells, himself of Serbian descent, traces the development of 'Christo-Slavic religious nationalism' in Serbia. This ideology, a blend of Christ's passion and the national trauma at Kosovo in 1389, when the Serbs were defeated by the Ottoman Turks in the legendary battle of Blackbird Field, identifies Slav Muslims not merely as apostates but as 'Christ killers'. Thus, Christo-Slavic nationalism underpinned the programme of ethnic annihilation and displacement launched in the summer of 1991, first against Croatia and then against the Croats and Muslims of Bosnia-Herzegovina. In similar fashion, Roman Catholic Christo-Slavic nationalists began their own assault on the Muslims in 1993. Religious prejudice also, Sells argues, lay behind the refusal to lift the arms embargo against the legitimate government of Bosnia, the Christian West being obsessed by the problem of Muslim immigrants and Islamic terrorism.

Islamic extremism was also a factor, though secondary, in the Bosnian conflict. Believing themselves to be participating in a Jihad against unbelievers, Sunni fundamentalist Mujahidin from Pakistan, Bangladesh and Sudan fought shoulder to shoulder with their beleaguered Muslim brethren, while sympathisers in Shi'ite Iran provided them with minor tactical weapons.

In 1995, stories began to multiply as to the horrific nature and extent of the 'ethnic cleansing' conducted by the Serbs – hundreds arbitrarily executed, with bodies dumped into mass graves – moved Dr Jonathan Sacks, Chief Rabbi in Britain, to join the Archbishop of Canterbury, Dr George Carey, and the Archbishop of Westminster, Cardinal Basil Hume, in a letter to *The Times* (14 July, 1995) condemning the 'evil actions' of those responsible.

On the same day, Dr Sacks denounced the 'politics of hatred' that had resurfaced in central Europe, saying that anti-Semitism – a 'human problem', not just a Jewish one – was identifiable in the revival of tribal identities throughout Europe. 'Racism,' he said, 'is a growing problem in the contemporary political environment. What is tragic from a Jewish perspective is that the lessons of the Holocaust do not seem to have been learnt.'

The bloody ethnic war in former Yugoslavia seemed to be ended by the US sponsored Dayton peace accords of November 1995, yet fears remained that the blood-letting would recommence. In March 1998 these fears were fulfilled when clashes occurred between the police of Serbia, dominant republic of the residual Yugoslavian federation, and ethnic Albanians of the southern Serbian province of Kosovo, leaving sixteen ethnic Albanians dead. Some responsibility may have lain with the ethnically Albanian Kosovo Liberation Army, fighting for independence for a province in which some 90% of the population were ethnic Albanians, and Muslims. At all events, as the year progressed fighting and killings continued, with mass graves of murdered ethnic Albanian men, women and children being uncovered.

A ceasefire accepted in October by Yugoslav president Slobodan Milosevic (a Serb), under threat of Nato air strikes, finally crumbled in January 1999 when 45 ethnic Albanians were massacred. Peace talks were arranged under further threat of Nato intervention, but Kosovo, being the original homeland of the Serbs and the seat of the Serbian Orthodox Church, and seen by Serb nationalists as their 'Holy Land' or 'Jerusalem', hopes of a settlement both amicable and permanent were not high.

The pessimism over Kosovo was vindicated when President Milosevic rejected the terms on offer at the end of the peace talks, although (or perhaps because) the ethnic Albanian delegation accepted them. Nightly bombing by Nato planes or missiles of strategic targets in Yugoslavia duly began on 24 March 1999 and continued with mounting intensity into the summer, to the accompaniment of 'ethnic cleansing' in Kosovo at the hands of Serb soldiers, para-militaries or police on a scale and of a savagery not seen in Europe since the Second World War, nearly a million ethnic Albanians having been driven from their homes and across the borders to adjacent countries by early June, with 500,000 displaced internally. Evidence mounted, especially following the acceptance of peace terms by Milosevic, that over 10,000 ethnic Albanians had been massacred.

The Nato intervention drew condemnation from Russia and China, and voices in the West expressed misgivings. In Britain, Lord Skidelsky argued in the June 1999 issue of *Prospect Magazine* that through Nato's action a new doctrine of international relations was being forged that would make the world a more dangerous place. He concluded with four perceptive assertions,

First, there is no international consensus on the standards expected of states in dealing with their own subjects or on the sanctions appropriate to breaches of agreed standards. Second, Nato failed to seek UN authorisation for its attack on Serbia because it knew it would not get it. Third, the bypassing of the UN by Nato sends a clear message to all countries that force, not law, governs international affairs. Fourth, if membership of the UN no longer protects states from invasion, all governments that can, will acquire weapons of mass destruction to deter or repel foreign invasion.

The illegality of the intervention was one argument raised against it; another was that however bad things had already become in Kosovo, the bombing made them worse by providing a cover for atrocities (*cf. The Independent on Sunday*, 28 March and 16 May 1999).

Ethnic or religious conflict, or 'cleansing', shows scant sign of abating, in Europe or anywhere else; indeed, it seems set to worsen, exacerbated by an ever-expanding world population. In some areas – Northern Ireland, Spain, Eastern Turkey, Algeria, Congo (former Zaire) and Sierra Leone, for example – there seems to be progress, but in Sudan, Eritrea/Ethiopia, Somalia, Angola, Iraq, Afghanistan and Sri Lanka there is currently no let up, and in Russia and other former Soviet states, in Iran, Pakistan, India (especially Kashmir), China, Indonesia, the Philippines, the USA and Western Europe ethnic or religiously motivated violence erupts spasmodically, with greater or lesser intensity. The general picture is bleak, and with fragmentation of old ethnic unions and contrived, if not forcible, creation of new ones the pattern of re-emerging ancient tribal hatreds seems established.

Ethnic/religious conflict is the most obviously disturbing trend as the third millennium dawns, yet growing world economic instability should perhaps alarm us more. Let us chart what has been happening over the last few years.

The summit held in June 1994 of the Group of Seven Leading Industrial Nations (G7) called for the renewal and revitalisation of global economic and financial institutions to assure the world of prosperity and well-being into the twenty-first century. A year later, when the G7 summit was held in Halifax, Nova Scotia, following a series of financial events which had shaken confidence in the health of the global financial system, and at a time when economists were voicing fears of a deterioration in world growth, no attempt had been made to reshape the world economic order.

The Halifax summit largely dismissed fears of recession or calls for a restructuring of the world financial system, falling back on 'reforms' of the existing system – prevention, wherever possible, of critical imbalances, and improved bail-out procedures. Yet that same year the financier George Soros felt constrained to give a sober warning, 'Economic theory needs to be fundamentally reconsidered. . . . The threat to free markets is part of a wider pattern. We are entering into a period of world disorder.' (*Soros on Soros: Staying Ahead of the Curve*, John Wiley, 1995). He proposed, by way of possible solution, 'a unified currency' – advice which may have been heeded by politicians in Europe, if not by others.

The Halifax proposal of improving the monitoring and surveillance powers of the International Monetary Fund (IMF), as also the idea floated of warning countries that if they got into a position like that of Mexico (recipient in 1994 of a $34 billion financial rescue package) they would have their debts forcibly rescheduled and assets forfeited, was to make all countries run ultra-safe monetary and fiscal policies. This unfortunately gave the financial markets even more power in relation to national governments, which in turn strengthened the tendency towards global deflation and mass unemployment.

The Halifax summit agreed on a 'Jobs Summit 2' in France for early 1996. But this meeting, held at Lille in April of that year, came up with no strategy for the creation of jobs, any more than had the first job summit held in Detroit in 1994. It simply concluded that unfettered competition was not the answer to the jobless problem.

The G7 conference held in Lyons at the end of June 1996 addressed primarily the problems raised by the globalisation of the world economy, particularly that of the debt trap into which the 20 or so poorest countries – mainly but not exclusively from sub-Saharan Africa – had fallen. Yet the G7 leaders could not agree to a suggestion that a proportion of IMF gold be sold for debt relief. (The idea was eventually taken up by the IMF and World Bank in April 1999.) The leaders faced a dilemma: while recognizing that economic laissez-faire was not the answer to the debt trap, they remained wedded to the belief that globalisation, with laissez-faire its foundation stone, was both inevitable and the best guarantor of prosperity and freedom.

At the beginning of February 1997 business leaders met in Davos, Switzerland, for the annual World Economic Forum. The only concern expressed was that financial turbulence could upset the 'benign' outlook for the world economy, such turbulence arising most probably in Europe, progressing towards monetary union, and in Japan, where the financial system was acknowledged to be fragile. A week later the finance ministers of G7 met in Berlin, their main concern the sharply falling yen. Their final communiqué sought to reassure,

> We believe that the major misalignments in exchange rates noted in our April 1995 communiqué have been corrected. . . . We believe that exchange rates should reflect economic fundamentals . . . and agreed to monitor developments in exchange markets, and co-operate as appropriate.

Despite such bland statements from economic summits, nervousness about the world's economic future, particularly fears of a major market crash and consequent global recession, remained. In the summer of 1997 the crisis broke.

Starting in Thailand, where the currency (the baht) plunged, it spread to Indonesia and South Korea. By 1998 nations with larger economies were feeling the strain. In May the Japanese yen and stock market slumped, amid a spate of news about bankruptcies. Fears mounted that market instability would suck China and Hong Kong into the turmoil, forcing them to devalue.

There was an uneasy feeling that for this downturn no end was in sight, the problem being no longer cyclical, but structural. Anxieties focused on the fact that the financial system was teetering under the burden of over $1000 billion in problem loans, dating back to the Japanese bubble economy of ten years before. There was talk of 'the Japanese death spiral': the Nikkei (Japanese stock market index) would go down, reducing the capital base of the banks; banks would then cut back lending to firms, leading to more business failures, which in turn would cause stocks to fall – and so on, down and down.

The world woke up to the gravity of the situation when, in late summer 1998, the Russian economy collapsed, the rouble going into free-fall and the regime defaulting on international loans. With government and private firms owing $194 billion of foreign debt to overseas governments and banks, the fear was that other countries badly affected by the downturn would follow suit. Anxiety was focused on Latin America – particularly Brazil, having the world's eighth largest economy. In November, it became necessary for the IMF, backed by the US Treasury, to arrange a $41.5 billion loan package for Brazil; yet in January 1999 the country was still forced to float its currency, the real, letting it drop sharply. World stockmarkets reacted with understandable nervousness.

The Russian economic crisis of 1998 we have referred to in Chapter II. It of course constituted but a single feature of a much wider scene of financial turmoil. What does and will that turmoil mean at the social level?

Crumbling pillars

Mass unemployment is the bogey of our time. The figures in 1998 for people out of work were: in the European Union, 18 million (officially unemployed); in the whole world, according to an International Labour Office (ILO) report of October 1998, 150 million (officially unemployed, mainly in industrial countries) – up from 120 million in the mid 1990s. If we add to the world figure some 900 million estimated by the ILO to be 'underemployed' (those who want to work more or are unable to earn a living wage) we reach a figure of over one billion. 'The global employment situation is grim and getting grimmer,' commented Michel Hansenne, director-general of the ILO.

The ILO report highlighted the fact that in Eastern Europe only Hungary and the Czech Republic had seen real wages approach pre-1989 levels, while generally they 'remain far lower than they were prior to the collapse of Communism'. There had accordingly been 'dramatic and painful declines in living standards' – most markedly in Russia.

The question of relative living standards is at the heart of today's economic crisis. In September 1998, in its annual Human Development Report, the United Nations called for urgent action to raise the living standards of the world's poor after disclosing that a billion people could not meet even their basic requirements, having failed to profit from the consumption boom of the previous twenty years. Gross inequalities were worsening, the Report said, with 20% of the global population accounting for 86% of consumption. Of the 4.4 billion people in developing countries, nearly 60% lacked basic sanitation, over 30% had no safe drinking water, 25% had inadequate housing and 20% were undernourished as well as having no access to reasonable health services. Meanwhile, the relief agency Oxfam was predicting the most dramatic reversal in human development the world had ever seen, destroying three decades of welfare gains; indeed, such reversal is already under way in Africa, according to a UN Development Programme report of April 1999, war, AIDS and debt having caused such economic and social havoc that it will take two generations simply to restore the situation to that of the 1970s.

Graeme Snooks, professor of economic history at the Australian National University in Canberra, has argued that inequality is a necessary phase of capitalism. In his book *The Dynamic Society* (Routledge, 1996), he maintains that the world is shaped by 'dynamic materialism' – a kind of 'survival of the fittest'. Human nature, he says, is unchanging, so any attempt to eliminate materialist man's primal urges could only be achieved through a global dictatorship, which would stifle economic growth through technology and ultimately lead to growth through the only other option –

war. Progress through dynamic materialism, however, is far from smooth: society may – as, for example, in Roman times – step over the brink into an abyss of chaos.

Another economist, Lester Thurow, argues that the West may even now be on the brink of a new Dark Age. In his book *The Future Of Capitalism: How Today's Economic Forces Shape Tomorrow's World* (Brealey, 1996) he points out that past societies which have existed successfully with inequality were undemocratic; democracy and inequality just do not mix. This, he says, has been recognised in the West for the past two centuries, with governments seeking to reduce inequality. Now, he warns, with income inequality being greater than at any time since records began, there are signs of social collapse.

To the informed the world seemed on the edge of the abyss in the fall of 1998. One of many alarmed commentators was François Chesnais. Writing in *Le Monde diplomatique* (September 1998; tr. Ed Emery), he said,

> Full blown depression will not be limited to Asia. Now the Russians are experiencing the misery that accompanies the collapse of economic activity; and they will soon be followed by the peoples of the Ukraine and other ex-Soviet republics. Nor will the process stop there: the peoples of Latin America will be the next victims of rentier and mafia-dominated global capitalism. . . . The pillars of the neo-liberal capitalist order are beginning to crumble one after another. Each time one goes down, the rest are put under even greater pressure. This is clear for Brazil, Argentina, Mexico, not to speak of Hong Kong and China. . . .

Chesnais sees the situation as recapitulating that of the 1930s, the financial crisis and global recession progressing simultaneously along three parallel, interdependent tracks. The first is deflation – the contraction in production, demand and trade, and the fall in prices – for which 'there are no known and easy remedies'. The second track 'is through the astronomical increase in bad debt, both private and public, held by the banking system'. He warned, 'When combined with political graft, the brutal spread of insolvency can bring the credit system to a halt, as in Indonesia and now in Russia'. The third track 'involves the close interconnectedness of the big stock markets and the transmission of funds from one to the other by increasingly nervous investors'. Chesnais' analysis, it may be noted, bears close resemblance to that of Will Hutton (see Chapter II).

What was done in late 1998, particularly by the world's leading industrial countries (G7), to counteract the worsening economic situation? Not a lot. After a series of meetings, the G7 nations urged a reduction of interest rates and generally expansionist policies (a change from the policy of fighting inflation), as well as the cleaning up of its banking system by Japan; they also proposed an emergency IMF borrowing facility at commercial terms for nations in special need – plans for which the IMF later disclosed. Some queried their policy of boosting demand by easing credit, recalling John Maynard Keynes' dictum that reducing interest rates in a flat economy is like 'pushing on a string'.

The World Economic Forum held in Davos in February 1999 had even less on offer. As Ben Laurance wrote (*The Guardian Weekly*, 14 February 1999),

> There was no attempt to deny it: the world *is* facing an economic crisis. A third of the world is in recession: no argument there. Some 1.3 billion people . . . have to try to live on less than $1 a day. There's no argument about that either. And few would be prepared to bet that the Brazilian crisis will not drag Latin America into the same economic abyss into which Asia has already tumbled. But that's where the consensus ended. . . . There was absolutely no agreement about what might actually be done to deal with this crisis.

What all now recognise is that individual nations can no longer act on their own in seeking to control their economies. Mr Tony Blair made the point in a speech in Australia to the News Corporation conference in July 1995,

> Globalisation is changing the nature of the nation-state as power becomes more diffuse and borders more porous. Technological change is reducing the power and capacity of government to control its domestic economy free from external influence. Free movement of currency means free movement of capital, which seeks the highest return possible.

For this reason alone – the fact of the global economy, the fact that national economies are inextricably interlinked, the fact that capital the creator knows no boundaries as hugely rich multi-national corporations grow in power, threatening the very foundation of democracy – we are likely eventually to see something very like world government. Economics and politics, as we know, cannot be disentangled. The present financial turmoil can only hasten the advent of such government. Though the world may seem for a while to weather the current crisis, another scenario is possible: spreading anarchy, or near-anarchy, such as we are already witnessing in Russia. If this transpires, the appeal of a single, centralised, dirigiste authority, a kind of global confederation, will become irresistible. It will seem the one bulwark against chaos.

A step in this direction has already been made – in Europe.

Imperium Romanum redivivum

In 1955 the members of the European Coal and Steel Community ('the Six') – Germany, France, Italy, Belgium, Luxembourg and the Netherlands – met in the Sicilian city of Messina and decided to work towards further economic integration. Three years later, the European Economic Community was established by the Treaty of Rome. On 22 January 1972 Prime Minister Edward Heath signed the Treaty on behalf of Britain, which officially entered the Community on 1 January 1973.

In December 1991 the Maastricht Treaty on a European Union (EU) laid down an 'irreversible' path to full economic and monetary union by member states of the European Community, with a single currency to be in place by 1999. The Treaty was ratified by all, problems of 'convergence' were overcome (with much help from Germany's Chancellor Kohl), and in May 1998 a meeting in Brussels of the leaders of the 15 member states approved the launch of the 'euro' for 1 January 1999; they also approved exchange rates for participating states and arrangements for a new European Central Bank, which would have the sole prerogative to alter interest rates over the euro-currency block. Eleven states were scheduled to join the European Monetary Union (EMU) in 1999: France, Germany, Italy, Spain, Portugal, the Netherlands, Belgium, Finland, Ireland, Austria, Luxembourg. Britain, Sweden and Denmark had already opted not to join in the first wave, while Greece was expected to do so as soon as it had met the Maastricht criteria.

As 1999 dawned, the euro was launched – and immediately there was talk of bringing forward the date for the issue of banknotes and coins.

The new currency's sponsors see it rivalling the US dollar. Jacques Santer, the then President of the European Commission, claimed at the World Economic Forum in Davos in March 1997 that the euro would become an alternative reserve currency, monetary union conferring on Europe superpower status. 'I am not Pangloss,' he said, 'I am looking at the empirical evidence.'

As a reserve currency the euro could become the focal point for an attempted restructuring of the world economic order, in response to economic turmoil produced by the deregulatory, laissez-faire approach of the present system. We have seen a massive fall, then gain, in the value of the dollar over the last few years, followed by an equally massive fall in the yen – which nevertheless strengthened again in late 1998. If the euro were to demonstrate more consistent strength, it would attract buyers in droves.

If currency turmoil continues, however, adversely affecting even the euro (it lost 15% of its value against the US dollar in the first six months of its life), investors will look for some other safe haven. They might even turn back to gold, making it effectively the common currency, just as it was for the civilised world in the last decades of the nineteenth century and up to 1914. There is no weakening in private sector demand worldwide, the market growing in the first quarter of 1999 by 62% over the same period of 1998.

A common world currency is no longer simply the stuff of fiction. As we have seen, George Soros considers 'a unified currency' a possible solution to global economic disorder. As a first step, he has counselled that the IMF 'take on more of the role of an international central bank' (*Newsweek*, 1 February 1999; *cf.* Soros' book *The Crisis of Global Capitalism*, Little, Brown, 1998). The need for a world central bank has also been identified by Will Hutton (*The Observer*, 4 October 1998),

Countries such as Russia or Brazil . . . need a central bank to act as lender of last resort when any individual economy is under speculative pressure. . . . If finance ministers can accept limits to sovereignty implied by a global intergovernmental regulator and allowing each other to inspect their regulatory agencies, establishing a world central bank is an obvious next step.

There is no doubt that monetary union in Europe will lead to political union through a federation of nation states; most 'Europhiliacs' have not disguised the fact that this has always been the aim. It could hardly be otherwise; history shows that every significant currency union that has not been backed by full political union has fallen apart – as with the nineteenth-century European silver franc. Martin Walker has written thus of monetary union (*The Guardian Weekly*, 12 April 1998),

Once the power to set interest rates is removed from nation states, their power to define their own economic policies, or even their own tax structures, will go into terminal decline. The new European Central Bank is the route through which federalism will come.

Federation will also involve the abolition of internal border controls, a common code of both civil law (already well under way) and criminal law, a common judiciary, common law enforcement and, in the end, a common army.

A call for the EU to be given an independent military capability was given on 19 June 1995 by the German Foreign Secretary, Herr Klaus Kinkel, who told the parliamentary assembly of the Western European Union (WEU) defence alliance in Paris that 'if the EU really intends to play an independent role in the sphere of foreign and security policy, it must be able to commit its own military means if necessary'. He declared that 'we cannot keep looking to the United States', proposing that the WEU defence alliance be merged into the EU (a plan now favoured by

France). A little later, on 1 September 1995, President Chirac made a significant offer, 'As it builds its defence, the European Union might wish the French [nuclear] deterrent to play a role in its security.' The same theme of European co-operation on defence and security was addressed in a meeting between the French President and British Prime Minister Tony Blair in December 1998, when the two leaders announced joint military and diplomatic responses to international crises by their respective countries – an initiative developed by Germany the following March in a proposal for a European defence identity, entailing standing military committees in Brussels with 15 army chiefs from the member states prepared – in consultation with their defence and foreign ministries – to deploy national troops in EU-led peace-keeping or peace-making operations. Two months later the president-designate of the European Commission, Romano Prodi, was calling unambiguously for a single European army.

The Balkan problem has highlighted as no other the need for the EU to have a meaningful military capability. It has exposed the impotence of UN forces when faced with anything beyond maintaining a *de facto* peace, and shown Nato – represented mainly by US firepower – to be the only viable police-keeping strikeforce in the area. The crisis in Kosovo accordingly became the catalyst that pushed the EU into adopting, at the Cologne summit of 1999, a formal European Security and Defence Identity (ESDI).

The former Yugoslavia is far from being the only dark cloud hovering around Europe, however. The situation in neighbouring Turkey, as in the Middle East as a whole, suffering increasingly from the ravages of militant Islamic or separatist extremism, testifies to the need for a European military corps capable of rapid deployment in areas threatened by violence – whether from bellicose foreign regimes, terrorists who have infiltrated from outside the region, or internal separatist minorities and insurgents.

There are other problems affecting Europe, directly or indirectly: the pressures of illegal immigration, nourished by an ever-expanding world population; the increase in criminal activity – corruption, racist violence, computer crime, electronic fraud, drug abuse, money laundering by the mafias (especially those emanating from Russia); the deepening 'environmental' crisis – inadequate food production (as in Russia), over-fishing, general pollution, nuclear waste disposal.

Searching for superman

In the face of such threats to social health and stability, the talk today is increasingly of the need for the 'smack of firm government', in the interests of order and 'control'. Democracy, people are beginning to argue, is secondary – a luxury, even.

If the European Union makes it necessary for its populace to be governed, in effect, by an unelected bureaucracy or 'civil service' called the European Commission, why worry? Politicians (people now protest) have not done much of a job; better a form of order imposed without popular mandate than no order at all. And if the authorities decide the maintenance of that order requires each citizen to hold (and perhaps carry at all times) an identity card, why complain? What difference can it make to carry another plastic card about? If, further, it is judged that effective monitoring of individuals necessitates the installation of cameras for closed-circuit video systems (already an estimated million in France alone) on street corners, in railway stations, banks, shopping malls, car parks and so on, what harm does it do so long as crime is kept under control? If, finally, the government feels it necessary to establish a DNA database, where everyone's 'genetic fingerprint' is stored, so what? Better to feel secure from random assault while being watched and controlled by a governmental 'Big Brother', than to walk in fear of your life while ostensibly enjoying freedom from state interference.

The erosion of individual liberty will continue as the pressures grow year by year. Europe, with its low birth rate, is unlikely to follow China in controlling the number of children born by penalising married couples who have more than one child, but it might one day, like China, pass a 'eugenics law' forbidding people with certain genetic diseases from marrying unless they submit to sterilisation or some form of long-term contraception. Euthanasia, too, may finally become legal, a move currently planned by the Dutch government. With the problem in Europe of an ever-growing proportion of elderly retired people creating a pensions 'time-bomb', there will be increasing pressure towards lightening the financial burden on the state in any way possible.

As problems multiply and life becomes – despite the 'control' – less and less secure, people will yearn for a way out. They will look for someone or something to rescue them from looming catastrophe. The situation will resemble that of Germany in the early 1930s, when the German people, enduring economic chaos and social turmoil under the Weimar Republic, largely welcomed Adolf Hitler as the 'strong man' who could pull things together. Nazism, let us recall, set a premium on social order, as well as care for the environment.

And Hitler still has a following – quite apart from skinheads and the political far-Right. On the fiftieth anniversary of Hitler's suicide (30 April 1945), Roger Boyes wrote from Bonn as follows (*The Times*, 1 May 1995),

Fifty years after Adolf Hitler's body was burned and buried in the garden of his Berlin Chancellory, the Nazi leader retains a grip on the popular imagination in Germany and the world.

Historians argue over Hitler's final moments in the bunker; teachers and politicians disagree over how to portray him in textbooks; an exhibition of Hitler portraits is viewed as dangerous; and publishers fret about publishing his turgid manifesto, *Mein Kampf*. Hitler compels attention. A picture of him or a swastika on the cover of a paperback can boost sales by 25% or more in the United States and many European countries. The sheer evil of the man fascinates. . . .

As world crisis deepens, some will conclude – like so many Germans of Hitler's day – that draconian measures imposed by inflexible political leadership constitute the one way out. Others will turn to personalities associated with the great religions for solace, and perhaps even material hope. There are, of course, those popular preachers whose stock in trade, besides prophecies on the future, is 'miracles of healing', and 'prosperity teaching', the idea that believers have a right to wealth. People from a traditional church background, however, are more likely to turn for inspiration to the Pope – if we go by the popularity of his book, already referred to, *Crossing the Threshold of Hope*, which sold over three million copies worldwide in 1994, or of a video released for Easter 1995 of His Holiness celebrating Mass from 'some of the world's most spectacular locations', for which a million copies were pre-ordered, or of the disc of his speeches in five languages issued in early 1999 to celebrate twenty years at the Holy See.

Orthodox Jews will be looking for the revelation of their coming *Moshiaoh*, or Messiah. In the early 1990s, members of the strongly Zionist Jewish 'Lubavitcher' sect hailed their rabbi Menachem Schneerson as Messiah – many of them looking for his resurrection following his death at the age of 92 in New York on 12 June 1994.

Those who have rejected traditional religious belief will be drawn to gurus from the East, or to one of the charismatic religious demagogues who arise in the West. An example of the former is His Holiness Maharashi Mahesh Yogi, founder of Transcendental Meditation, who in double-page newspaper advertisements in 1992 invited 'the people and government of Great Britain to bring their national constitution into alliance with the Constitution of the Universe' (the 'Source of all Order and Harmony'), which he claimed to have discovered through Vedic science. Two examples of the latter – unbalanced individuals, as so often – are the Rev. Jim Jones, who in November 1978 commanded his followers to lie down and die, with the result that 900 men, women and children committed mass suicide in Guyana, and David Koresh, who, styling himself Christ, headed the Branch Davidian cult – until he and 74 others died when his headquarters at Waco, Texas, were destroyed by fire while under siege by federal agents on 19 April 1993, two years to the day before the Oklahoma bombing.

We are living, as never before, in an era of 'prophets' and 'messiahs'; the trend is likely to strengthen.

We can expect to see all branches of the Church moving towards unity in the coming millennium. In May 1995 Pope John Paul's encyclical *Ut Unum Sint* ('that they all may be one') called for a rapprochement between the world's 958 million Roman Catholics and 200 million Orthodox Christians. The goal for the two churches, separated since the Great Schism of 1054, was stated to be full inter-communion by the end of the millennium. More remarkably, if an article in the newspaper *La Voce* (July 1994) is to be believed, a 1994 Consistery of Cardinals discussed a letter calling for a Third Vatican Council, dedicated to Christian unity, to take place in the year 2000. The letter proposed 'a council of Roman Catholic, Protestant and Orthodox figures to discuss main topics leading to unification'. The implication is that Roman Catholic reunion with Orthodoxy is a precursor to communion with other denominations.

A unified, 'universal' Church of this nature will be less and less dogmatic in its teaching – witness the Vatican's recent derogation of Satan, in exorcist rituals, to an impersonal 'cause of evil'. The Church will wish, in particular, to co-operate with other major religions – Judaism, Islam, Buddhism, and Hinduism, in the main – on environmental, social and political issues of the day. We can expect its espousal of the feminist cause to gather momentum, its theology and language reflecting the view that sees the Godhead more and more as 'Mother' as well as (or rather than) 'Father'. This development will be encouraged by the enhanced prominence of the Virgin Mary, in line with Pope John Paul's own commitment to the Marian cult. Appeal will increasingly be made to the Virgin (as in the new Vatican exorcist rituals), new 'visions' of her will occur and old ones will be publicised.

The Church will lay fresh emphasis on the veneration of 'saints' and their relics, as well as on paranormal phenomena, partly in order to attract some of the growing numbers of people interested in New Age types of religious experience. The 'Christian' religious scene will, indeed, tend to resemble that of the Roman Empire, with its 'gods many and lords many', the greatest of whom was the goddess Diana – whom Romans identified with the Greek Artemis, ancient mother goddess of Asia Minor worshipped by the Ephesians. Just how far this process has already gone is documented by Alan Morrison in his book *The Serpent and the Cross: Religious Corruption in an Evil Age* (K and M Books, 1994). Above all, the institutional Church of the coming millennium is likely to redouble its efforts to boost its influence and power, while preaching a humanitarian gospel of 'peace'.

The borders of the European Union are likely to expand to incorporate the six new countries, Estonia, Poland, the Czech Republic, Hungary, Slovenia and Cyprus (assuming a Greek-Turkish Cypriot settlement), currently engaged in accession negotiations with the 15 existing members. The more distant target of 26 members may be reached sooner than expected. The question mark over Turkey's application remains, but the problems on both sides will be surmounted if membership is seen as important for strategic reasons, bearing in mind the country's close ties with Israel. The latter itself and the Palestinians, together with Jordan, may eventually be brought in as members, or at least as associate members, the ultimate problem of Jerusalem having been 'solved' by a Treaty jointly brokered by the European Union and the United States of America, probably supported by the Vatican.

The Holy City may well be designated the 'religious capital' of the world, international at the spiritual level while actually under Israeli sovereignty, the Treaty delineating its status being difficult to interpret (if not intentionally ambiguous) as it strives to please all parties. The Palestinians will be pressed to sign in return for guarantees as to their 'virtual statehood'. Jordan may find it politic to give its approval, but we can expect Syria to demur, with Egypt – anxious to appear non-aligned – perhaps remaining aloof. Anti-Zionist Muslim nations like Iran, Iraq, Sudan and Libya are likely to denounce the Treaty, a move that will further confirm their status in the eyes of the West as 'pariahs'.

The United States of America, Canada and the Latin American nations will tend to draw closer, especially economically, probably forming a currency union; they, together with Australia and New Zealand, will maintain close political ties with the European Union, possibly formalising these in protocols guaranteeing economic, political and military co-operation in a 'New Western Alliance'. The nations of the New World, peopled quite largely by immigrants from Europe, will wish to perpetuate their links with the cradle of Western civilisation.

Despite efforts by world leaders, however, social and economic conditions will deteriorate globally year by year (most disastrously in Africa), with racist and other types of crime rife, acts of terrorism multiplying, public order increasingly difficult to maintain as drug barons consolidate their power, and brush-fire wars proliferating both between and within smaller nations. Food shortages – already afflicting other parts of the world – may begin to affect Europe and North America.

On the macro-political front, the 'New Western Alliance' will be disturbed by the growing military strength of the nations of the East – especially Japan, China, and India – who will possibly have concluded a non-agression pact. Meanwhile, the Middle East settlement will show signs of imploding, freshly threatened by Islamic extremist violence within, and the increasingly bellicose stance of the 'pariah' Muslim states without. The popular hope, in the West, will be for some quasi-miraculous delivery from a disaster that threatens to engulf civilisation. In the end, the answer will be found. Or rather, he will appear – just as the world's problems seem insuperable. The new leader will be hailed as saviour. . . .

A dark figure

It is not my purpose formally to argue the case for the accuracy of predictions contained in the Christian (and Jewish) scriptures. Suffice to say that the Jesus who foresaw, and foretold, the fall of Jerusalem in A.D. 70 also foresaw a more distant future.

Since the late nineteenth century, of course, the majority of scholars have denied that Jesus predicted the fall of Jerusalem, arguing that the three 'synoptic' gospels which contain this prediction (Matthew, Mark and Luke) were written after A.D. 70 – despite the lack of internal (textual) or external evidence for such a view. More recent scholarship, however, sees the synoptic gospels as having been written well before the fall of Jerusalem, perhaps only 10 to 25 years after Jesus' death (see Wenham, John, *Redating Matthew, Mark and Luke*, Hodder and Stoughton, 1991; *cf*. Robinson, J.A.T. *Redating the New Testament*, SCM, 1976). The German papyrologist Carsten Thiede has further adduced evidence, from his examination and analysis of fragments of papyrus from Qumran, in Palestine, and from Egypt, that Mark's gospel was written no later than A.D. 50, a copy of it being sealed by A.D. 68 into one of the Qumran caves (which housed the 'Dead Sea Scrolls'), and that Matthew's gospel was written by the mid-sixties at the latest. (See Thiede, C.P., *The Earliest Gospel Manuscript?*, Paternoster, 1992; *and* Thiede, C.P. and M. d'Ancona, *The Jesus Papyrus*, Weidenfeld and Nicolson, 1996).

We may therefore assume that what Jesus is recorded in the gospels as having said about the future is what he actually said, and can accordingly give his 'outline of history', commencing with the fall of Jerusalem. This is what Jesus said (Lk 21:6, 20, 23b, 24; Mt 24:5-18, 21,22; Lk 21:25, 26) when some of his followers had been admiring the Temple stonework:

> As for these things which you see, the days will come when there shall not be left here one stone upon another that will not be thrown down. . . . But when you see Jerusalem surrounded by armies, then know that its desolation has come near. . . . Great distress shall be upon the earth and wrath upon this people [the Jews]; they will fall by the edge of the sword, and be led captive

among all nations; and Jerusalem will be trodden down by the Gentiles, until the times of the Gentiles are fulfilled. . . . Many will come in my name, saying, "I am the Christ," and they will lead many astray. And you will hear of wars and rumours of wars; see that you are not alarmed; for this must take place, but the end is not yet. For nation will rise against nation, and kingdom against kingdom, and there will be famines and earthquakes in various places; all this is but the beginning of the sufferings.

Then they will deliver you up to tribulation, and put you to death; and you will be hated by all nations for my name's sake. And then many will fall away, and betray one another, and hate one another. And many false prophets will arise and lead many astray. And because wickedness is multiplied, most men's love will grow cold. But he who endures to the end will be saved. And this gospel of the kingdom will be preached throughout the whole world, as a testimony to all nations; and then the end will come.

So when you see the desolating sacrilege spoken of by the prophet Daniel, standing in the holy place (let the reader understand), then let those who are in Judea flee to the mountains; let him who is on the housetop not go down to take what is in his house; and let him who is in the field not turn back to take his mantle. . . . For then there will be great tribulation, such as has not been from the beginning of the world until now, no, and never will be. And if those days had not been shortened, no human being would be saved; but for the sake of the elect those days will be shortened. . . . And there will be signs in sun and moon and stars, and upon the earth distress of nations in perplexity at the roaring of the sea and the waves, men fainting with fear and with foreboding of what is coming on the world, for the powers of the heavens will be shaken. . . .

Jesus' words are not original; they reflect, as we are told, the teaching of 'the prophet Daniel' (several scrolls of the book of Daniel were found at Qumran); they also reflect the teaching of other prophets and writers of the Jewish scriptures (the Old Testament), men such as Isaiah, Jeremiah, Ezekiel, Joel, Amos, Micah, Zechariah, Malachi. Jesus did not foresee a world journeying into light after he had left it in physical form; rather he saw it being engulfed, eventually, in darkness. And he saw – like Daniel, and like his friend and disciple John – the world being one day drawn after a world leader, a false 'saviour', who would turn out to be more than people had bargained for (cf. Jn 5:43b).

Daniel records a vision in which he saw four great beasts, symbolising 'four kings who shall arise out of the earth' (Dan. 7:17). Thus he writes

(Dan. 7:2-8; *cf.* Dan. 2:31-43):

> I saw in my vision by night, and behold, the four winds of heaven were stirring up the great sea. And four great beasts came up out of the sea, different from one another. The first was like a lion and had eagle's wings. Then as I looked its wings were plucked off, and it was lifted up from the ground and made to stand upon two feet like a man; and the mind of a man was given to it. And behold, another beast, a second one, like a bear. It was raised up on one side; it had three ribs in its mouth between its teeth; and it was told, "Arise, devour much flesh." After this I looked, and lo, another, like a leopard, with four wings of a bird on its back; and the beast had four heads; and dominion was given to it. After this I saw in the night visions, and behold, a fourth beast, terrible and dreadful and exceedingly strong; and it had great iron teeth; it devoured and broke in pieces, and stamped the residue with its feet. It was different from all the beasts that were before it; and it had ten horns. I considered the horns, and behold, there came up among them another horn, a little one, before which three of the first horns were plucked up by the roots; and behold, in this horn were eyes like the eyes of a man, and a mouth speaking great things.

It is not difficult to identify these 'kings'. They are four successive world empires, which arise from the 'great sea' – that is, from among the restless nations and peoples (a common piece of symbolism in the Bible; *cf.* Is. 17:12,13a; Ps. 65.7; Lk. 21:25). The winged lion was (as archaeology testifies) an apt symbol for the Babylonian empire under Nebuchadrezzar, indicating his might and the speed of his initial conquests. The empire was quickly extended to include Chaldea, Assyria, Arabia, Syria, Palestine, Egypt and Tyre. These conquests were suddenly arrested, however, and the Babylonian ferocity and cruelty were superseded by a more tolerant and human attitude. The bear was a fitting symbol for the Medo-Persian empire, which though inferior to the Babylonian in power, civilization and nobility, was more covetous and voracious. The three ribs in its mouth probably refer to Babylon, Lydia and Egypt, countries which fell prey to the gluttonous, all-consuming rapacity of the Persian power. The four-winged, four-headed leopard is a remarkably appropriate representation of the Grecian empire. Alexander the Great ascended the throne of Macedon at the age of twenty. Almost immediately he proceeded rapidly (as if winged) to extend his territory; Medes, Parthians, Hyrcanians, Bactrians and Sogdians were subdued in lightning succession, after which the conqueror crossed the Indus to invade India. Alexander died young, and his vast empire was divided up between his four principal generals (the 'four heads') – Cassanda taking Macedon and Greece, Seleucus taking Syria and Upper Asia, Lysimachus becoming ruler of Asia Minor and Thrace, while Ptolemy took Egypt, Palestine and Arabia.

The fourth beast can only refer to the Roman empire, whose far-reaching dominion, plundering, and iron rule of conquered nations distinguished it from its predecessors. Its unnamed representative beast had 'ten horns', which Daniel tells us are 'ten kings'. By analogy with the four heads of the leopard (four 'kings'), the ten kings should be considered contemporaneous. Such never existed in the Roman empire of old – which appears to present a problem. But let us go further.

From among the ten horns there came up, in Daniel's vision, 'another horn, a little one'. 'As I looked,' Daniel explains, 'this horn made war with the saints, and prevailed over them, until the Ancient of Days came, and judgement was given for the saints of the Most High, and the time came when the saints received the kingdom.' Daniel then tells us that this horn is in fact one more king, who 'shall be different from the former ones, and shall put down three kings. He shall speak words against the Most High, and shall wear out the saints of the Most High, and shall think to change the times and the law; and they shall be given into his hand for a time, two times, and half a time. But . . . his dominion shall be taken away, to be consumed and destroyed to the end.' (Dan.7:21, 22, 24-26).

The ten kings, and the eleventh, are in Daniel's scheme to reign at the time of the end, when God himself (the 'Ancient of Days') intervenes. In other words, the fourth world empire, the Roman, is to last right up to the moment of this denouement. Which is as we might expect, for in truth the Roman empire has never really died; it has merely changed its form – first being split into two under Valentinian I, who in A.D. 364 gave the eastern part, based on Constantinople, to his brother Valens, then being broken up into smaller parts, yet with a thread of continuity always persisting as various rulers – Byzantine emperors, Charlemagne, certain Popes, the Russian Czars, Napoleon, the Kaiser, Hitler, and now (implicitly) leaders of the European Union – have claimed to be its true heirs. (*Cf.* Dan. 2:40-43).

So the ten kings, and the eleventh, are yet future. Daniel's 'fourth beast' would appear to correspond to the ten-horned, seven-headed 'beast' of John's book of Revelation (13:1). The eleventh dark figure resembles the 'beast' (Rev. 13:5-18) who utters blasphemies, makes war on the saints, whose number is 666 (see Chapter V) and whose image is set up – probably the 'desolating sacrilege' of which Jesus spoke.

That same Jesus is our hope against all such evil.

IV: Rex Quondam Rexque Futurus

It is said that the words inscribed on the grave of King Arthur were these: 'Rex quondam rexque futurus', 'Once and future king.'

No figure of any national legend has attracted to itself such a mass of interpretative detail as Arthur of England. Beginning from a historical leader who genuinely achieved a period of peace and order in the stormy wars between Celts and Anglo-Saxons, this figure attracted to its story great and good elements from largely Christian sources on all sides. By the genius of Sir Thomas Malory, the legend in its final form represented Christianity in a form meaningful to a nation by that time compounded of Celts, Anglo-Saxons and Normans. For over 500 years from A.D. 1130 this national myth exercised an extraordinary influence. Not that Arthur was seen as a prophet, or in any way perfect. But he represented the ideal leader – coming to the rescue, beset by enemies without and his own conscience within. He is essentially Christian. Born like his master under the cloud of doubtful parentage, he is tempted and (in his case) falls into the temptation, but from that time climbs slowly up to a scene in which he becomes himself the righteous sufferer. Nor is that the end, for according to those words on his tomb his people will see him again.

Why speak of Arthur, who represents only a national ideal? Because he exemplifies most perfectly the perennial inclination of men and women of every nation, age and clime to find their own saviour-figure. Italian peasants found such a figure in their patron saint, who would set them free when they prayed to him. The Franks and their successors saw in Charlemagne something of the same delivering strong man. Teutonic races made Balder the White a larger-then-life focus for their national aspirations. Greeks once vested in Lord Byron the same semi-divine quality, his death at Missolonghi while supporting their cause of independence being seen as a sacrifice of huge significance. In modern times it is probably Che Guevara, who 'fought in Guatemala, conquered in Cuba, and died in Bolivia', whose memory has attracted the aura of an almost superhuman hero. But we must move from type to antitype. For Jesus of Nazareth is the reality behind the dreams. The 'desire of nations', he is the true 'once and future king'.

Suffering servant

Few seriously doubt that in 4 B.C. or a little earlier a child was born in Bethlehem, in the Roman province of Judea, who was to become in early manhood the object of local adulation. For a few years – probably no more than three – during that restless period Jesus of Nazareth seemed to the common people amongst whom he moved to be the hero for whom they had been waiting. Here, at last, was the one who would lead them against the hated foreign oppressor. Here was the promised saviour.

It was not only Jews, however, who had been waiting for such a figure. The Roman historian Suetonius tells us in his *Lives of the Caesars* (*Vespasian*, iv) that the whole of the East expected the deliverer from Roman dominion to come from Judea. Others further afield had had 'dreams' of the appearance one day of a superhuman leader, a man-god, a magnificent king who would bestow every blessing upon his subjects and worshippers. In his classic study *The Golden Bough* (Macmillan, 1890), J.G. Frazer shows how in almost every ancient culture this idea prevailed. To such a man-god sacrifice might be made; or the man-god himself might offer sacrifice; or the superhuman figure might yield himself to sacrificial death (by means of a proxy, done to death by the man-god's followers, as in ancient Mexico), only to rise again, bringing with him in mystic union all his devotees. The hero becomes in fact a dying-rising god, conquering death for himself and for those who adhere to him. Such was Osiris, the great god of ancient Egypt, whose annual death and resurrection have been celebrated in so many lands.

Some have believed that the prevalence of these man-god figures in the ancient world calls in question the historicity of the life and death of Jesus. Such thinking is illogical. For the story of Jesus is in truth that of a man who was himself moved by just such 'dreams', considering himself the one reality behind them, their single ultimate fulfilment. The dreams that inspired him, however, were not stories handed down by oracular priests or woven into obscure religious rituals, but carefully written records of events or accounts of the lives of individuals from the history of his own people of Israel.

There were many prototypes for the one antitype, Jesus. There was 'Joseph and his amazing technicolour dreamcoat' – Joseph, sold into slavery by his own brethren, considered dead, yet appearing later as viceroy of Egypt, able to save those same brethren, and his and their father, from starvation; there was Moses, also rejected by his own people, later to become their deliverer from the tyranny of Pharaoh, finally to become their lawgiver; there was Joshua (the name but a variant of 'Jesus', meaning 'saviour'), who led the people across Jordan and so into the promised land; there was David, outlawed and persecuted by King Saul, yet anointed by the prophet Samuel to be Saul's successor – as in due course he became, setting up his royal throne in Jerusalem; there was the strange figure in the book of Isaiah, 'the righteous one, my servant', a kind of personification of Israel, whose task was to bear the griefs and sins of others through his own suffering and death (Is. 52:13 – 53:12); there was Jeremiah, yet another servant of God rejected by his own people (because he prophesied not peace but judgement), who foresaw a time when God would 'make a new covenant with the house of Israel and the house of Judah', saying 'I will put my law within them, and I will write it upon their hearts; and I will be their God, and they shall be my people' (Jer. 31:31,33).

Jesus was well acquainted with this history and the prophetic writings even as a boy (Lk 2:46,47; *cf.* Mt 13:54-56); small wonder that he found inspiration in what he read. But there was something else: the growing sense – partly, maybe, as a result of hints from his mother about the circumstances of his birth – that he had been singled out to play an unprecedented role on earth, to be himself the consummation of all those dreams, those visions, and to be true heir to the heroes of his nation.

So Jesus' ministry commenced, when he was 'about thirty years of age' (Lk 3:23), with his baptism at the hands of his cousin, John. The latter initially demurred at baptizing such a charismatic figure, his baptism being one of repentance, a symbolic washing away of people's sins in the waters of the Jordan; John must have wondered what sin this 'Lamb of God' could possibly need to be cleansed of. 'I need to be baptised by you, and do you come to me?' he asked. Jesus' reply is significant, 'Let it be so now; for thus it is fitting for us to fulfil all righteousness.' (Mt 3:15). From the very first, Jesus was moulding himself to a pre-ordained pattern. He was acting a role, one of humility. He was to be mankind's servant.

The nature of Jesus' role is clarified further by his next experience – one of severe temptation in the wilderness of Judea. The way this happened may well be described for us in symbolic rather than literal terms; his temptations probably stand for mental battles he endured throughout his ministry, though supremely at its outset. We need not doubt, however, that the account came from the lips of Jesus, for the highly pictorial language is just what we would expect from one who was a master story-teller.

Three options lay before Jesus, all of which he rejected. He refused to use his special powers – as yet untested – to make stones into bread, giving as his reason (in words addressed to the devil), 'Man shall not live by bread alone, but by every word that proceeds from the mouth of God.' (Mt 4:4). At one level he was simply refusing to pander to his own hunger;

at a deeper level he was voicing his conviction that the provision of spiritual sustenance is far more important than that of bodily sustenance. In other words, he was rejecting an interpretation of his mission that would mean devoting himself to the work of providing for man's physical needs.

The second temptation (according to Matthew) was that of challenging God to support and preserve him whatever he chose to do – like throwing himself off a pinnacle of the Temple. The dismissal of this idea not only represented the refusal to prove his messianic identity to himself, but also a refusal to prove it before the world by performing some extraordinary feat.

Jesus' third temptation is perhaps the most significant. Satan, we are told, 'showed him all the kingdoms of the world and the glory of them; and said to him, "All these I will give you, if you will fall down and worship me."' (Mt 4:8,9). C.H. Dodd explains what this means (*The Founder of Christianity*, Collins, 1971), 'He might gain power by "doing homage to the devil" . . . or, in realistic terms, exploiting the latent forces of violence to wrest from Rome the liberation of his people.' As with the other two temptations, Jesus brushed aside the seductive notion – even when, later, people tried 'by force to make him king' (Jn 6:14,15).

Jesus clearly ruled out an interpretation of his ministry that would mean his becoming a social reformer, public hero, or political revolutionary. This has been disputed by some, who refer to passages from the gospels which they present (after much reading between the lines) as 'evidence' for Jesus' political activism. An incident that occurred shortly after the temptation in the wilderness is occasionally cited.

Returning from the wilderness, Jesus came into Galilee, where he taught in the synagogues, being 'glorified by all' (Lk 4:15). He then (4:16-21),

> came to Nazareth, where he had been brought up; and went to the synagogue, as his custom was, on the sabbath day. And he stood up to read; and there was given to him the book of the prophet Isaiah. He opened the book and found the place where it was written, 'The Spirit of the Lord is upon me, because he has anointed me to preach good news to the poor. He has sent me to proclaim release to the captives and recovering of sight to the blind, to set at liberty those who are oppressed, to proclaim the acceptable year of the Lord.' And he closed the book, and gave it back to the attendant, and sat down; and the eyes of all in the synagogue were fixed on him. And he began to say to them, 'Today this scripture has been fulfilled in your hearing.'

This has been seen as Jesus' declaration of a political manifesto. Leaving aside the fact that after his reading and electrifying announcement

– which certainly constituted a claim to messianic status – 'all in the synagogue were filled with wrath', dragging him outside the city and up to the brow of a hill in order to throw him over, there is a small but vital detail in this account. Jesus breaks off his reading from Isaiah (61:1,2a) in the middle of a sentence, omitting the words 'the day of vengeance of our God'. In other words, he deliberately draws a line between the messianic mission of preaching the good news of release to those in bondage, sight to the blind, liberty to the oppressed, on the one hand, and 'the day of vengeance', on the other. All the former tasks he fulfilled, in his own way, since he ministered to the 'poor' by proclaiming that they could find forgiveness and eternal life through him, healing many from their ailments (including blindness), releasing others from demonic possession, and even (we are told) raising one or two from the dead. What he refrained from doing was taking up a sword of vengeance against the foreign oppressor or against those from among his own people who opposed him.

Not that Jesus suggested there would never be such a 'day of vengeance'. He warned that 'days of vengeance, to fulfil all that is written' would occur after his departure – when Jerusalem, far from being delivered from the Romans, 'the Gentiles', would actually be destroyed and 'trodden down' by them (Lk 21:22,24). And he looked further still to the coming of the 'Son of Man' (a title he reserved for himself; *cf.* Lk 5:23,24) 'in a cloud with power and great glory' (Lk 21: 27), when he would judge the nations (Mt 25:31-33). A day for political activism (to put it mildly) *was* coming, but it was not to be yet, not to be part of his mission in first-century Palestine.

Some time after his unpleasant experience in the synagogue at Nazareth, public acclaim for Jesus reached its height (a commentary, perhaps, on how fickle public opinion can be), but the angry reaction of those in the synagogue indicates how early in his ministry Jesus had to face rejection. This of course is what he had chosen in assuming the Servant role described by Isaiah. All use of force he ruled out; he had, for the moment, chosen the way of unconditional love, which never resists violence physically.

In my book *What on Earth?* I argue this in greater detail, showing how Jesus' interpretation of his role as Messiah was consistently apolitical to the last – right up to the moment of his death. It is, indeed, the manner of his end that proves the point conclusively, the fact that he accepted death, when it came through the betrayal of a friend, the plottings of enemies, and the weakness of the Roman governor, without making any attempt to resist it. As he told the governor, Pontius Pilate, 'My kingdom is not of this world: if my kingdom were this world, then would my servants fight, that I should not be delivered to the Jews: but now is my kingdom not from hence.' (Jn 18:36, RV).

Jesus steadfastly took upon himself the role of Suffering Servant. It was, in a sense, the role of 'outsider'. His people, as a whole, spurned him, and he was crucified outside the gate of Jerusalem. At that point he was, truly, the personification of the nation. The role that had apparently first been appointed for the people corporately had been funnelled into this one son of Israel. Isaiah's words about 'the righteous one, my servant' are perfectly fulfilled in him (Is. 53:3,8,9,12).

> He was despised and rejected by men; a man of sorrows, and acquainted with grief; and as one from whom men hide their faces he was despised, and we esteemed him not . . . cut off out of the land of the living, stricken for the transgression of my people. . . . They made his grave with the wicked and with a rich man in his death, although he had done no violence, and there was no deceit in his mouth. . . . He poured out his soul to death, and was numbered with the transgressors; yet he bore the sin of many, and made intercession for the transgressors.

Jesus 'poured out his soul to death'; yet he would have been aware of words from the same prophecy that indicated that he, 'the righteous one', would not be swallowed up forever. For Isaiah also says (Is. 53:10-12),

> When he [my servant] makes himself an offering for sin, he shall see his offspring, he shall prolong his days . . . he shall see the fruit of the travail of his soul and be satisfied. . . . Therefore I will divide him a portion with the great, and he shall divide the spoil with the strong.

He would also have known some other words of scripture – penned, it was said, by David himself (Psalm 16:10, RV),

> My heart is glad, and my glory rejoiceth: my flesh also shall dwell in safety. For thou wilt not leave my soul to Sheol; neither wilt thou suffer thine holy one to see corruption.

According to the gospel writers, Jesus was confident that prophecies such as these about life beyond the grave for God's righteous servant or 'holy one' would be fulfilled as completely as those about his death; he knew that 'Sheol' (place of the departed; or 'Hades', in Greek) could not hold him.

It is recorded on several occasions that Jesus predicted his resurrection (*e.g.* Mt 16:21). The apostle Peter, referring to the same Davidic psalm, explained a few weeks later to the crowds in Jerusalem exactly what had happened. He cried (Acts 2:29-31),

> Brethren, I may say to you confidently of the patriarch David that he both died and was buried, and his tomb is with us to this day. Being

therefore a prophet, and knowing that God had sworn with an oath to him that he would set one of his descendants upon his throne, he foresaw and spoke of the resurrection of the Christ, that he was not abandoned to Hades, nor did his flesh see corruption. This Jesus God raised up, and of that we are all witnesses.

It is beyond the scope of this book comprehensively to argue the case for the truth of the claim that Jesus rose from the dead. It can, however, be pointed out that there are significant flaws in the thesis of those who suggest that the dead body of Jesus did not disappear miraculously from the tomb in which it was placed, not least the psychological difficulty of believing that the early disciples were able – without irrefutable evidence of Jesus' resurrection – to preach, convince others about, and die for such an astonishing and improbable story. The disciples' claim, recorded in the gospels and elsewhere in the New Testament, to have met the risen Jesus is the most obvious form of evidence; but it would be a mistake to underestimate the significance, for those early Christians, of the empty tomb. Peter refers to it obliquely. More importantly, no one seems to have tried refuting what he said by producing the body of Jesus, or pointing to another tomb in which the body remained. Suggestions that the disciples themselves stole away the body, or that, following the trauma of the crucifixion, Jesus revived in the tomb and by appearing to his disciples in his natural body convinced them he had risen, cannot be taken seriously.

So Jesus, the Servant, became the risen Lord, his earthly mission accomplished. The continuation of his work was now, as he had taught, in the hands of his earthly followers, and all those who would later join them. He left behind him no blueprint for society, for he had never spoken of social reform, let alone political revolution. He had been, at his first appearing in the world, concerned solely with the welfare of individuals – their relationship with God, and, flowing from this, their attitude to their neighbour. If the moral enlightenment and transformation of such individuals should lead indirectly to an improvement in society, well and good. Such a result would always, however, be secondary, a by-product of the immediate objective.

Jesus offered no solution to chaos in this age beyond calling men and women to repent of their sins and put their trust in him; it has been the mission of his followers ever since to call men and women to a like repentance and faith, and thus to service of God and mankind. The world has materially benefited from this, certainly; yet, barring the miracle of global repentance, the worldwide situation will become increasingly dire.

Jesus has another role, however, besides that of Suffering Servant. It is the role he will adopt at his second appearing on earth, when he comes again 'in a cloud, with power and great glory' (Lk 21:27). There is no ultimate 'solution' to the problems that bedevil our world beyond the unilateral solution that will be imposed by God at that time.

Son of David

Matthew's gospel begins, 'The book of the genealogy of Jesus Christ, the son of David, the son of Abraham'. After the genealogy itself (Mt 1:1-16), there is an account of 'the birth of Jesus Christ', beginning with the message of an angel to 'Joseph, son of David', when Mary (his 'betrothed') had been found 'with child of the Holy Spirit' (1:18-21). Luke also stresses the Davidic descent of Jesus, giving his genealogy (3:23-38). He records a message of the angel Gabriel to Mary, in which it is promised of Jesus, 'The Lord God will give to him the throne of his father David, and he will reign over the house of Jacob for ever' (1:32,33). All of which is strange when we find that both writers have given Jesus' genealogy back to David through *Joseph*, who was in reality – they both insist – not his fleshly father. What is more, their two genealogies 'through Joseph' are quite different.

It is clear from the rest of the New Testament that Jesus' Davidic descent 'according to the flesh' was considered crucial (Acts 2:25-36; 13:22,23; Rom. 1:3; II Tim. 2:8), so we should expect to find Mary's genealogy recorded somewhere. Could it be that one of the evangelists is in fact tracing Jesus' descent from David through Mary? It is stretching credibility too far to imagine that either of them included a fictional genealogy in his gospel. Among the Jews of Jesus' day genealogies would generally have been known and prized – just as they were until recently among Muslims of northern Sudan, some of whom would know them by heart.

One of the gospel genealogies must surely be that of Mary. J. S. Wright (*Our Mysterious God*, Marshalls, 1983)argues that it is preserved by Luke, bearing in mind that the early chapters of Luke's gospel are written from Mary's point of view. He writes (*Our Mysterious God*, Marshalls, 1983),

> In Luke, Joseph is the son of Heli, whereas in Matthew's gospel he is described as the son of Jacob. Let us suppose, then, that Mary's father was Heli. Mary had a sister; we are told that 'standing by the cross of Jesus were his mother, and his mother's sister.
>
> We are nowhere told of a brother. If, therefore, Heli had two daughters only, the line, which was always traced through the male line, would have died out. The regulations quoted in Numbers 27:1-11 and 36:1-9, were that, when daughters only survived, their possessions and their family name required a male relative, or at least someone of the same tribe, to carry them on. Even if

Joseph was not a (near) relative of Mary, he was of the line of David, and, in marrying her, he carried on the line of Heli, thus becoming the son of Heli.

Wright's interpretation is probably correct, though there have been other satisfactory explanations as to how the apparently discrepant genealogies can both be purveying historical truth. (*Cf.* Blair, H.A., *A Stranger in the House: the astonishing gospel*, Darton, Longman and Todd, 1963; he finds evidence that it may have been Matthew who preserved Mary's genealogy, an early copyist's error having crept into the text.) The important point to establish is that Jesus was a descendant of David 'according to the flesh'. In this regard we should appreciate the point that Joseph very probably was a kinsman of Mary, since people in those days tended to marry relatives; this in itself makes Mary likely to have been of Davidic descent.

Why was Jesus' descent from David so important? Precisely because of the promise that as the messianic son of David he would one day sit on David's throne – a promise recorded not only by Luke, but also by many of the prophets (Is. 9:7; Jer. 23:5; 30:9; 33:15; Ezek. 34:23; Hos. 3:5; *et al.*).

Peter once said to Jesus, 'We have left everything and followed you. What then shall we have?' Jesus replied, 'Truly, I say to you, in the new world, when the Son of man shall sit on his glorious throne, you who have followed me will also sit on twelve thrones, judging the twelve tribes of Israel' (Mt 19:27,28). Jesus did not doubt that beyond the destruction of Jerusalem (the 'days of vengeance'), beyond the 'desolating sacrilege' and the 'great tribulation' following it, life would go on. That is to say, the world would not end; it would, rather, be renewed. The word translated 'new world' in the RSV means literally 'regeneration' or 'restoration to life'. As it is used by Jesus (who would actually have been speaking in Aramaic) it may refer to the resurrection of the disciples as individuals as much as to the regeneration of the world. Nevertheless, whatever the word's precise significance, Jesus makes it clear that the 'Son of man' (he himself) will one day sit on the throne of Israel – still a nation of twelve tribes.

Jesus is the once *and future* king. As son of David, he remains the true king of Israel, one day to come into his earthly inheritance. Which is a statement many Christians would challenge.

In the mainstream churches it is unfashionable to suggest that Israel considered corporately, Israel as a nation, still has a unique place in God's purposes for the world. It is not 'politically correct' to claim that the physical descendants of Jacob/Israel remain in any sense 'God's chosen people'.

St Paul, needless to say, was not bothered about being politically correct.

In his letter to the Christians at Rome he is particularly concerned to show how the offspring of Israel remain 'God's people', declaring that 'God has not rejected his people whom he foreknew' (Rom. 11:2; *cf.* 11:28b,29). He draws attention to God's acceptance of individual Israelites (or Jews) like himself as Christian believers. Such are 'at the present time . . . a remnant, chosen by grace', or 'the elect' (11:5,7); as for 'the rest', they have been 'hardened' (11:7). Yet he assures us that as well as this, Israel *as a whole* will one day believe the Gospel, thereby bringing untold blessing to the world (11:12,15,24). He sums up (11:25,26):

> I want you to understand this mystery, brethren: a hardening has come upon part of Israel, until the full number of the Gentiles come in, and so all Israel will be saved; as it is written, 'The Deliverer will come from Zion, he will banish ungodliness from Jacob'.

'The Deliverer will come from Zion. . . . ' Paul carefully echoes a sentence from the Jewish scriptures (Is. 59:20). For him the Deliverer is Israel's Messiah, son of David, Son of man – in other words, Jesus, destined to ascend his royal seat in Zion, which is Jerusalem.

In Isaiah the Deliverer is 'the Lord', who will 'repay wrath to his adversaries, requital to his enemies', and who 'will come like a rushing stream, which the wind of the Lord drives' (59:18,19). There follows (Is. 60) a hymn to 'the City of the Lord, the Zion of the Holy One of Israel':

> Arise, shine; for your light has come, and the glory of the Lord has risen upon you. For behold, darkness shall cover the earth, and thick darkness the peoples; but the Lord will arise upon you, and his glory will be seen upon you. And nations shall come to your light, and kings to the brightness of your rising. Lift up your eyes round about, and see; they all gather together, they come to you; your sons shall come from far, and your daughters shall be carried in the arms. Then you shall see and be radiant, your heart shall thrill and rejoice; because the abundance of the sea shall be turned to you, the wealth of the nations shall come to you. A multitude of camels shall cover you, the young camels of Midian and Ephah; all those from Sheba shall come. They shall bring gold and frankincense, and shall proclaim the praise of the Lord. All the flocks of Kedar shall be gathered to you, the rams of Nebaioth shall minister to you; they shall come up with acceptance on my altar, and I will glorify my glorious house. . . . Foreigners shall build up your walls, and their kings shall minister to you; for in my wrath I smote you, but in my favour I have had mercy on you. . . . Your sun shall no more go down, nor your moon withdraw itself; for the Lord will be your everlasting light, and your days of mourning shall be ended. Your people shall all be

righteous; they shall possess the land for ever, the shoot of my planting, the work of my hands, that I might be glorified. . . . I am the Lord; in its time I will hasten it.

How far can we 'spiritualise' this Old Testament prophecy, and many others like it? Do we simply extract from such passages purely personal comfort as we apply the promises metaphorically to ourselves? How far do we argue that, though the prophets clearly considered that what they were saying would one day be fulfilled literally, their words cannot be taken at their face value in the light of the new, Christian revelation? Do we conclude that the promises made by God through his prophets to the sons of Israel about a literal and glorious restoration of their national fortunes (centred on Jerusalem) have now been rescinded?

The followers of Jesus once put a question to him that is highly relevant; it is recorded by Luke in his second volume of Christian history, the Acts of the Apostles. Affirming that Jesus had 'presented himself alive after his passion by many proofs, appearing to them [the apostles] during forty days, and speaking of the kingdom of God' (1:3), Luke goes on to tell us how on one such occasion the apostles asked him, 'Lord, will you at this time restore the kingdom to Israel?' (1:6). He answered, 'It is not for you to know the times or seasons which the Father has fixed by his own authority.' (1:7). Here was no swift rebuke for suggesting that there might still be a national future for Israel, no careful explanation that the old dispensation, the old 'covenant', had been entirely superseded by the new. On the contrary, far from denying that the kingdom would one day be restored to Israel, Jesus merely pointed out to the apostles that it was none of their business to know when God was going to put his plans into effect – including, by implication, his plan to restore the kingdom to Israel.

The closest personal friend of Jesus was probably John, son of Zebedee – who may have been his cousin on his mother's side. The latter was the writer of the fourth gospel, three New Testament epistles, and the book of Revelation. After his resurrection, Jesus said of John in answer to a question by Peter, 'If it is my will that he remain until I come, what is that to you? Follow me!' (Jn 21:22). John did not of course live to see Jesus' coming again, nor (John tells us) did he think his master's reply to Peter meant that he would. It is appropriate, nevertheless, that it was to John, in exile much later on the island of Patmos, that a vision of Jesus' coming in glory was granted. He speaks of it in his book of Revelation.

The book of Revelation, which deals with all the events of the last days, is full of colourful imagery and symbolism – as is inevitable in any attempt to describe a vision. The depiction of Jesus' return in glory, though true, is not intended to be taken completely literally. This is how John (19:11-15) sees it,

Then I saw heaven opened, and behold, a white horse! He who sat upon it is called Faithful and True, and in righteousness he judges and makes war. His eyes are like flame of fire, and on his head are many diadems; and he has a name inscribed which no one knows but himself. He is clad in a robe dipped in blood, and the name by which he is called is The Word of God. And the armies of heaven, arrayed in fine linen, white and pure, followed him on white horses. From his mouth issues a sharp sword with which to smite the nations, and he will rule them with a rod of iron; he will tread the wine press of the fury of the wrath of God the Almighty.

John goes on to refer to Jesus' enemies at this time, 'I saw the beast and the kings of the earth with their armies gathered to make war against him who sits upon the horse and against his army.' (19:19). The 'kings of the earth' had been assembled, he has already told us, by 'demonic spirits', at 'the place which is called in Hebrew Armageddon' (16:14,16). Confronted by the armies of heaven, 'the beast' (and his 'false prophet') are vanquished, together with the kings and their armies, and there follows a period of 'a thousand years' during which 'the dragon, that ancient serpent, who is the Devil and Satan' is bound, 'that he should deceive the nations no more, till the thousand years were ended' (20:2,3). The vision continues (20:4),

Then I saw thrones, and seated on them were those to whom judgement was committed. Also I saw the souls of those who had been beheaded for their testimony to Jesus and for the word of God, and who had not worshipped the beast or its image and had not received its mark on their foreheads or their hands. They came to life again, and reigned with Christ a thousand years.

John's thought and language in Revelation echo that of the Old Testament prophets, especially Isaiah, who uses similar imagery in speaking of the last battle (66:15,16,24) and Israel's Messiah. Of the latter, 'a root from the stump of Jesse' (Jesse was David's father), he says (11:3b-5),

He shall not judge by what his eyes see, or decide by what his ears hear; but with righteousness he shall judge the poor, and decide with equity for the meek of the earth; and he shall smite the earth with the rod of his mouth, and with the breath of his lips shall he slay the wicked.

John also echoes the book of Daniel, particularly in his description of the glorified Jesus returning to earth (*cf.* Dan. 7:9), as also in his depiction of the final dark night of world history that precedes Jesus' return. (We shall look more closely at this 'dark night' in the next chapter.) And his language sometimes reflects the prophecies of Ezekiel.

So we have Old Testament prophets, Jesus, the gospel writers, Paul – who was the main writer of the New Testament apart from the evangelists – all believing and teaching that there is going to be a climax of history, when God himself, in the person of the divine Messiah of Israel, will step onto the world stage to usher in his own 'New World Order'. That Order will be one in which God's 'ancient people', the sons of Israel, will once again be caught up into the channel of his purposes. There is no warrant, if we are to be honest and consistent in our approach to scripture, for dismissing as invalid the promises of a global 'golden age', under the suzerainty of the son of David, with Jerusalem (and Israel) at the centre.

At the end of the Old Testament we find the book of the prophet Malachi – the last in the long line of Hebrew prophets. Among the concluding sentences are these (4:1,2),

> The day comes, burning like an oven, when all the arrogant and all evildoers will be stubble; the day that comes shall burn them up, says the Lord of hosts, so that it will leave them neither root nor branch. But for you who fear my name the sun of righteousness shall rise, with healing in its wings.

The promise is unequivocal. It is of a coming day of the Lord, when evil will be judged and consumed, but when all those who fear God – Jew and Gentile alike – will be vindicated, and healed.

Last Adam

Healing is what the concept of a 'millennial kingdom' is really about.

The prophet Ezekiel foresaw a perfected land of Israel in this kingdom (Ezek. 40-48). In a vision (47:6-9,12, RV), a guide shows him a river of healing waters,

> He brought me, and caused me to return to the bank of the river. Now when I had returned, behold, upon the bank of the river were very many trees on the one side and on the other. Then said he unto me, 'These waters issue forth toward the eastern region, and shall go down into the Arabah: and they shall go toward the sea; into the sea shall the waters go which were made to issue forth; and the waters shall be healed. And it shall come to pass, that every living creature which swarmeth, in every place whither the rivers come, shall live; and there shall be a very great multitude of fish: for these waters are come thither, and the waters of the sea shall be healed, and everything shall live whithersoever the river cometh. . . . And by the river upon the bank thereof, on this side and on that side, shall grow every tree for meat, whose leaf

shall not wither, neither shall the fruit thereof fail: it shall bring
forth new fruit every month, because the waters thereof issue out
of the sanctuary: and the fruit thereof shall be for meat, and the
leaf thereof for healing.

In God's plan, scripture tells us, there is to be a restoration of paradise,
of Eden. As Adam was given the responsibility for tending the land and
caring for – and naming – the animals in Eden, so the 'Last Adam' (as St
Paul describes Jesus; I Cor. 15:45) must oversee a 'healing' of the plant
and animal world in the millenial kingdom, the second Eden. Ezekiel is
not the only prophet to see this time as one of blessing for the natural
world; Isaiah says the same. In the section from which we have already
quoted words about Messiah ruling 'with righteousness' (11:1-5), there
is a passage (11:6-9) about a renewed animal kingdom,

The wolf shall dwell with the lamb, and the leopard shall lie down
with the kid, and the calf and the lion and the fatling together,
and a little child shall lead them. The cow and the bear shall feed;
their young shall lie down together; and the lion shall eat straw
like the ox. The sucking child shall play over the hole of the asp,
and the weaned child shall put his hand on the adder's den. They
shall not hurt or destroy in all my holy mountain; for the earth
shall be full of the knowledge of the Lord as the waters cover the
sea.

Isaiah speaks elsewhere (35:1; 41:18b,19, RV) of a newly flourishing
plant kingdom,

The wilderness and the parched land shall be glad; and the desert
shall rejoice, and blossom as the rose. It shall blossom abundantly,
and rejoice even with joy and singing. . . . I will make the
wilderness a pool of water, and the dry lands springs of water. I
will plant in the wilderness the cedar, the acacia tree, and the
myrtle, and the oil tree; I will set in the desert the fir tree, the
plane and the cypress together.

While making due allowance for necessary symbolism in such
prophecies about the future (as indeed for descriptions of Eden), there is
no doubt that the writers saw a time when nature would be 'healed',
renewed, transformed. This is as it should be; there is a rightness about
the planet enjoying its sabbath, after the current despoliation – which
may yet worsen. Should the natural creation suffer for ever?

St Paul tells us that it surely does 'suffer', but that in the day when
humanity is finally glorified (becoming children of God – like Jesus, the
Son of God) it too will be transfigured. 'We know that the whole creation
has been groaning in travail together until now,' he writes (Rom. 8:22).
For which reason, he explains, it 'waits with eager longing for the

revealing of the sons of God; for the creation was subjected to futility, not of its own will but by the will of him who subjected it in hope; because the creation itself will be set free from its bondage to decay and obtain the glorious liberty of the children of God.' (Rom. 8:19-21).

The millennial kingdom is to be the world's jubilee. It is the great fallow period, when savagery will be banished from nature and outlawed from mankind. It is the time when – under a benevolent theocracy – physical endeavour of every description will burgeon and flourish. Above all, it will be for humanity a time of peace – outward, material peace such as men have for so long sought in vain, as well as the quiet, inward kind that can be maintained even when the world crumbles about you.

The prophet Micah (echoing Isaiah) once summarised the millennial vision. As we ponder his words (4:1-4), we must decide whether they are 'just poetry', or whether – though poetic diction is the medium – they describe what will one day transpire. If Jesus is what he claimed to be, can they fail eventually to be fulfilled?

It shall come to pass in the latter days that the mountain of the house of the Lord shall be established as the highest of the mountains, and shall be raised up above the hills; and peoples shall flow to it, and many nations shall come and say: "Come, let us go up to the mountain of the Lord, to the house of the God of Jacob; that he may teach us his ways and we may walk in his paths." For out of Zion shall go forth the law, and the word of the Lord from Jerusalem. He shall judge between many peoples, and shall decide for strong nations afar off; and they shall beat their swords into plowshares, and their spears into pruning hooks; nation shall not lift up sword against nation, neither shall they learn war any more; but they shall sit every man under his vine and under his fig tree, and none shall make them afraid; for the mouth of the Lord of hosts has spoken.

V: Jacob's Trouble

Faithful few

The history of the people of Israel is a history of returns. These have sometimes been literal returns, but more often they have been moral. Time and again the people have wandered from the truth as revealed to them through their leaders or prophets, time and again it has seemed God will disown them for their unfaithfulness, yet each time the divine tutor has refused to write them off. From their (religious) history contained in scripture we find that the main reason for this has been that however faithless they may sometimes have been there has always been a faithful 'remnant'.

The first clear rebellion against God occurred about a year after Moses had won them their freedom from the bondage of Pharaoh and led them out of Egypt (Exodus 1-15). The people refused to believe that they could, under Moses and with God's help, conquer the land promised to them (Numbers 13,14). The result was that they spent forty years wandering in the wilderness – until the whole generation of adults who had come from Egypt had expired. Only Caleb and Joshua, who had been fully prepared to enter Canaan and who thus constituted a tiny 'remnant', together with the children of the rebels, finally entered the promised land. Moses was allowed a glimpse, but no more.

The people's infidelity did not cease when they had settled in Canaan. It is recorded in the book of Judges that during their first period in Canaan 'the people of Israel did what was evil in the sight of the Lord. . . . they went after other gods, from among the gods of the peoples who were round about them . . . and served the Baals and the Ashtaroth. So the anger of the Lord was kindled against Israel, and he gave them over to plunderers. . . . Then the Lord raised up judges who saved them out of the power of those who plundered them. And yet they did not listen to their judges . . . ' (2:11-14,16,17). The theme is of a wayward people saved by the faith of the few.

In the first book of Samuel we read of the last judge over Israel, Samuel, whom 'all Israel from Dan to Beersheba knew . . . was established as a prophet of the Lord' (I Sam. 3:20). On one occasion, when the ark of the covenant was sent back to Israel by the Philistines after they had captured it (they had grown to fear it, following several unaccountable disasters),

Samuel challenged the people of Israel to return to the Lord. They duly 'put away the Baals and the Ashtaroth, and . . . served the Lord only' (7:3,4). Following this, 'the Philistines were subdued . . . and the hand of the Lord was against the Philistines all the days of Samuel' (7:13).

When Samuel grew old, 'he made his sons judges over Israel. . . . Yet his sons did not walk in his ways, but turned aside after gain; they took bribes and perverted justice. Then all the elders of Israel gathered together and came to Samuel at Ramah, and said to him, "Behold, you are old and your sons do not walk in your ways; now appoint for us a king to govern us like all the nations."' (8:1,3-5). Thus it was that first Saul, son of Kish, was anointed king by Samuel, then David – after Saul had disobeyed the command of God given through Samuel.

David, son of Jesse the Bethlehemite, became king of Israel in 1011/10 B.C., but it was only after many troubles, for Saul had tried desperately to kill him. David 'did what was right in the eyes of the Lord, and did not turn aside from anything that he commanded him all the days of his life, except in the matter of Uriah the Hittite' (I Kings 15:5). Under David the kingdom of Israel was established and extended. It was extended further under Solomon, his son and successor, Israel becoming a relatively powerful nation among those of the area, as recorded in the first book of Kings.

Solomon's riches greatly impressed the Queen of Sheba (I Kings 10:1-13). Israel's power and prosperity had in fact reached a peak – appropriately enough, for Solomon 'loved the Lord, walking in the statutes of David his father' (3:3). Yet he also 'loved many foreign women', who, when he was old, 'turned away his heart after other gods. . . . Ashtoreth the goddess of the Sidonians, and . . . Milcom the abomination of the Ammonites' (11:4,5).

Israel's glory was accordingly short-lived. We read that 'Jeroboam, the son of Nebat, an Ephraimite of Zeredah, a servant of Solomon . . . very able . . . lifted up his hand against the king. . . . Solomon sought therefore to kill Jeroboam; but Jeroboam arose, and fled into Egypt, to Shishak king of Egypt, and was in Egypt until the death of Solomon.' (11:26,28,40). Returning from Egypt, Jeroboam persuaded most of the people to throw in their lot with him instead of with Rehoboam, Solomon's unpopular son and heir.

Jeroboam became king over a new, northern kingdom of 'Israel', making his capital in Shechem, 'in the hill country of Ephraim'; he set up calves of gold in Bethel and Dan, designating other idolatrous shrines on high places and appointing his own priesthood (12:16,19,20a,25-31). Rehoboam, however, retained a royal seat in Jerusalem, from where he governed 'the people of Israel who dwelt in the cities of Judah'; these were for the most part members of the two tribes of Judah and Benjamin (12:20b,21). So the Davidic kingdom of all Israel was divided into northern 'Israel' and southern 'Judah'.

Some time later 'Elijah the Tishbite' became a prophet in the northern kingdom (I Kings 17). This was in the time of Ahab, son and successor of Omri, founder of the dynasty. Ahab reigned as seventh king of Israel for twenty-two years (*circa* 874-852 B.C.), marrying the notorious Jezebel, daughter of Ethbaal, king of Tyre and Sidon and priest of the goddess Astarte (Hebrew 'Ashtoreth'; plural form, 'Ashtaroth').

Ahab denounced Elijah to his face as 'troubler of Israel'. The latter responded, 'I have not troubled Israel; but you have, and your father's house, because you have forsaken the commandments of the Lord and followed the Baals.' (18:17,18). There followed a contest on Mount Carmel, in which Elijah challenged the prophets of Baal to demonstrate the power of their god by calling him to send down fire on their offering to him. They failed, while Elijah successfully called down 'the fire of the Lord' upon the offering prepared for the God of Israel. The assembled people duly acknowledged that 'the Lord, he is God', and the prophets of Baal were seized and slain (18:30-40).

Ahab the king then told his wife Jezebel what had happened, and she sent messengers to Elijah threatening to kill him. He was afraid, and fled into the wilderness, journeying on until he reached Mount Horeb, where the Lord met him, asking in 'a still small voice' what he was doing. Elijah replied,

> The people of Israel have forsaken thy covenant, thrown down
> thy altars, and slain thy prophets with the sword; and I, even I
> only, am left; and they seek my life, to take it away.

The Lord told him to return, assuring him that many of his enemies would be slain in a coming upheaval. He added, 'Yet I will leave seven thousand in Israel, all the knees that have not bowed to Baal, and every mouth that has not kissed him.' (19:1-18). Once again we find a 'faithful remnant' in God's largely apostate people.

The northern kingdom of Israel as a whole never turned back in faith to 'the Lord'. Soon, indeed, it was being threatened by a new power in the region – that of Assyria.

Ancient Assyria had been a small area around the Tigris river (now northern Iraq, far eastern Turkey and a little of eastern Syria), but it grew into an empire stretching from the eastern Mediterranean to modern Iran. In 725 B.C. the king of Assyria, Shalmaneser, invaded Israel and placed Samaria – its capital at the time – under siege. It finally fell to his successor, Sargon, in 722 B.C.. Most if not all of the northern Israelites were carried captive to Assyria, being replaced by people from elsewhere in the

Assyrian empire; these settlers in due course half-heartedly embraced Israel's religion. The Israelites who had been carried captive to Assyria never returned.

What of the southern kingdom of Judah?

In 701 B.C. king Sennacherib of Assyria overwhelmed Judah and laid siege to Jerusalem. The prophet Isaiah delivered a broadside at Sennacherib, predicting that because of his arrogance he too would be judged, while Jerusalem, and Judah's God-fearing king Hezekiah, would survive unscathed (Is. 10:5-19; 36; 37). His prediction was fulfilled when the Assyrian army, encamped around Jerusalem, was decimated by a mysterious plague, forcing Sennacherib to withdraw to his own land. There it was, in 681 B.C., that the Assyrian king was murdered by his own sons while worshipping in the temple of Nisroch in Nineveh.

Isaiah likens Assyria to a glorious forest which will one day be devoured by fire from 'the light of Israel . . . his Holy One' (10:17). In other words, the tables are to be turned completely: Israel, having been almost annihilated, will – in the person of Israel's 'light', her 'Holy One' – wreak just retribution. Isaiah then goes on to predict that at the time of Assyria's humbling a 'remnant of Israel' will, having up to then relied upon treacherous foreign allies, turn back to 'the Lord, the Holy One of Israel' as their one true helper. 'A remnant will return', he repeats (10:20,21).

Has there been a fulfilment of these words – in the sense, particularly, of a heartfelt return to faith in 'the Lord'?

A 'remnant of the house of Judah' was certainly delivered from the mighty Sennacherib, as we have seen. As Isaiah had prophesied (37:31,32), this remnant took root downward, and bore fruit upward, trusting afresh in their God. Yet just over a century later, as a result of further apostasy denounced by Jeremiah (Jer. 5:20 – 6:26; 17:1-4), Judah was invaded by the Babylonian armies of Nebuchadrezzar. Jerusalem was looted and all but the poor of the land were taken captive to Babylon. In around 537 B.C. a 'remnant' of these captives returned under the terms of a decree of Cyrus, king of Persia, who had captured Babylon two years earlier. These Jews, who had never forgotten Jerusalem (*cf.* Psalm 137), also renewed their vows to God.

Yet Isaiah speaks of a more comprehensive return. This is confirmed in the passage (Chapter 11) which immediately follows the prediction of Assyria's downfall and the promise of a returning remnant. The passage constitutes a description of the coming Messiah, 'a root from the stump of Jesse', to which we referred in the last chapter. After describing Messiah and his righteous rule over the nations, the prophecy continues (11:11-12),

In that day the Lord will extend his hand yet a second time to recover the remnant which is left of his people from Assyria, from Egypt, from Pathros, from Ethiopia, from Elam, from Shinar, from Hamath, and from the coastlands of the sea. He will raise an ensign for the nations, and will assemble the outcasts of Israel, and gather the dispersed of Judah from the four quarters of the earth. Isaiah's words were echoed later by Jeremiah (30:3; 31:8,31,33),

Days are coming, says the Lord, when I will restore the fortunes of my people, Israel and Judah. . . . I will bring them back to the land which I gave to their fathers, and they shall take possession of it. . . . I will bring them from the north country, and gather them from the farthest parts of the earth. . . . I will make a new covenant with the house of Israel and the house of Judah. . . . I will put my law within them, and I will write it upon their hearts; and I will be their God, and they shall be my people.

Clearly, there has not yet been a total fulfilment of either Isaiah's or Jeremiah's words about a returning remnant.

Many seek to see such a fulfilment in the life and ministry of Jesus in first-century Palestine. We immediately recall those God-fearing Jews at the time of Jesus' birth: his own earthly parents, Joseph and Mary; Mary's kinswoman Elizabeth and her husband Zechariah (parents of John the Baptist); old Simeon and the 'prophetess Anna, daughter of Phanuel, of the tribe of Asher', giving thanks at the appearance of the child Jesus in the Temple (Lk 1-2:36). Then we have Jesus' own followers, the first disciples, as well as Jews who joined the Church after his resurrection.

'A remnant, chosen by grace' thus existed in Jesus' own day, and immediately thereafter (Rom. 11:5); Paul, we have seen, points out that he himself was a part of it. All those faithful sons or daughters of Israel experienced something of the 'new covenant' of which Jeremiah spoke, for the law of God was written by his Spirit in their hearts .

Yet Jeremiah tells us that the promise of the 'new covenant' will one day be fulfilled in the context of a national regathering of 'Israel and Judah . . . to the land which I gave to their fathers'. Such a return has yet to occur. There has in our day, of course, been a physical return to the land of some of the sons of Judah and Benjamin ('Jews', whose ancestors inhabited Judah). Among them are a number of descendants of the other ten tribes, who formed the northern kingdom of Israel (sometimes designated 'Ephraim'). Perhaps Jews of modern times can be seen as representing all twelve tribes – though neither the words of Jeremiah nor of Isaiah would appear to allow this (*cf.* also Ezekiel 37:15-22).

What we have not seen is a 'return' of all Israel to their Lord as he was and is revealed in Jesus, their Messiah. How will this come about?

Lord of the Flies

William Golding's masterpiece *Lord of the Flies* (Faber, 1954) has at its heart a 'beast'. That beast can be identified with several things: there is the ghastly moving bulbous thing that Simon confronts on the mountainside; there is Jack, whose behaviour becomes sickeningly beast-like; there is the pig's head on a stick (most obviously the 'Lord of the Flies'); and there is finally that less tangible 'beast' within all the boys (mostly cathedral choristers, ironically) who persecute Simon, Piggy and Ralph.

In ancient Israel there were also 'beasts'; they were referred to as 'Baals', a 'Baal' meaning literally 'master', 'possessor' or 'husband'. When the Israelites entered Canaan they found every piece of land had its own deity, its 'owner'. There were thus many 'Baals'. The Baal cults challenged the worship of the God of Israel – 'Yahweh', or 'Jehovah' – throughout Israelite history, the incident on Mount Carmel being the outstanding battle between the two. The particular Baal favoured by Ahab was Melqart, the seat of whose worship was at Tyre, Jezebel's home. The God of Ekron was 'Baalzebub', or 'Lord of the Flies'. It is possible that the name 'Baalzebub' was a mocking Hebrew alteration of 'Baalzebul', which means 'Lord of the High Place'.

In the New Testament we find the Pharisees accosting Jesus with the accusation that he was casting out devils by 'Beelzebub [*i.e.* Baalzebub, or Baalzebul] the prince of the devils'. Jesus (Mt 12:24-27, RV) made an astute reply,

> Every kingdom divided against itself is brought to desolation; and every city or house divided against itself shall not stand: and if Satan casteth out Satan, he is divided against himself; how then shall his kingdom stand? And if I by Beelzebub cast out devils, by whom do your sons cast them out? Therefore shall they be your judges.

Jesus in fact sees behind this 'Beelzebub', this 'prince of devils', none other than the real power for evil in the universe, Satan – the angelic being who, he says elsewhere, once fell 'like lightning from heaven' (Lk 10:18; *cf.* Isaiah 14:12-15; Ezekiel 28:12-19).

That power for evil, and his manifestation in the world as a grotesque 'lord of the flies', or 'beast', is what we meet in the prophecies of Isaiah, Daniel, Jesus, John and Paul concerning the consummation of this age, the 'end of history'.

There have been prototypes for the 'beast' of the end time – called also 'antichrist' by John (I Jn 2:18), or 'the man of sin' by Paul (II Thess. 2:3, RV). The first was the Pharaoh in Egypt who defied God as represented before him in the person of Moses. Then there was Goliath, the Philistine giant, who opposed the armies of Israel amassed under Saul, offering himself in single combat and then boastfully dismissing the challenge of the youthful David – only to be ignominiously slain by a stone from the latter's sling (I Sam. 17:49). A much closer prototype was furnished by the Seleucid king Antiochus IV Epiphanes, who in the early second-century B.C. ruled 'Syria' – at that time an empire that included eastern Asia Minor, Syria, Palestine, ancient Assyria and Babylonia, and on into Persia to the borders of India. He is described in some detail by Daniel.

Daniel writes (11:20-35),

> Then . . . shall arise a contemptible person to whom royal majesty has not been given; he shall come in without warning and obtain the kingdom by flatteries. . . . Forces from him shall appear and profane the temple and fortress, and shall take away the continual burnt offering. And they shall set up the abomination that makes desolate. . . . But the people who know their God shall stand firm and take action . . . though they shall fall by the sword and flame, by captivity and plunder, for some days. . . . Some of those who are wise shall fall, to refine and to cleanse them and to make them white, until the time of the end, for it is yet for the time appointed.

What Daniel says tallies with what we know of Antiochus IV Epiphanes, who secured his place on the Seleucid throne by Machiavellian cunning. When king Seleucus Philopater was murdered, and his heir (a boy of eleven) was being held in Rome, Heliodorus seized the throne. His title was at once disputed by Ptolemy Philometor of Egypt, while Antiochus set about a strategy to obtain the throne for himself. Antiochus first 'flattered' Eumenes, King of Pergamum, and his brother Attalus, in order to gain their financial and military assistance; then he 'flattered' the Syrians with a promise of clemency and less taxation; finally, he employed the same technique with the Romans, sending ambassadors to court their favour with a rich present and the payment of arrears of tribute.

Antiochus' vicious treatment of his Palestinian province occurred after the Romans had intervened during his third campaign against 'the king of the south', Ptolemy Philometor of Egypt, who had been joined by his brother. The Romans forced Antiochus, in humiliating fashion, to withdraw. He had already given special favours to apostate Jews (led by one Menelaus) who were seeking to hellenize the people and do away with religious rites; now he sent Apollonius with 22,000 soldiers to destroy Jerusalem. Thousands were massacred, worshippers were murdered, the Temple rituals forbidden and the city itself pillaged and set on fire.

Antiochus then published a decree requiring all to conform to the Greek religion and announcing that the Temple was henceforth to be dedicated to Jupiter Olympus, with whom he identified himself. Finally, on 25 December 167 B.C., he erected a heathen altar on the Jewish altar of burnt offering.

Many Jews capitulated, but a 'remnant' remained faithful, suffering much in consequence. Very soon the Maccabean uprising – helped by 'the wise', who imparted spiritual instruction to the masses – threw off the foreign yoke. The national religion was reinstated in 164 B.C..

At this point in Daniel's prophecy we encounter something perplexing. Following the words 'the time of the end, for it is yet for the time appointed', we are told more about 'the king'. Yet it is impossible to find parallels from the life of Antiochus IV to what is written about this figure. 'The king,' we read, 'shall do according to his will; he shall exalt himself and magnify himself above every god, and shall speak astonishing things against the God of gods . . . ' (11:36). This is true up to a point of Antiochus IV, as is some further description. But the narrative goes on, 'Those who acknowledge him he shall magnify with honour. He shall make them rulers over many and shall divide the land for a price.' (11:39). Such a policy was never implemented by Antiochus IV, who in fact died on campaign in Media in 164 B.C.. 'The land', incidentally, must refer (from the perspective of the Jewish writer) to Palestine, land of God's people.

The description of events continues (11:40-45),

> At the time of the end the king of the south shall attack him; but the king of the north shall rush upon him like a whirlwind, with chariots and horsemen, and with many ships; and he shall come into countries and shall overflow and pass through. He shall come into the glorious land. And tens of thousands shall fall. . . . He shall stretch out his hand against the countries, and the land of Egypt shall not escape . . . the Libyans and the Ethiopians shall follow in his train. But tidings from the east and the north shall alarm him, and he shall go forth with great fury to exterminate and utterly destroy many. And he shall pitch his palatial tents between the sea and the glorious holy mountain; yet he shall come to his end, with none to help him.

As the 'king of the north' is to make an onslaught upon 'him', that is, upon the king who presumptuously magnifies himself 'above every god', the latter cannot be identified with Antiochus IV, who is himself 'the king of the north', being in the same dynasty as Antiochus III (or, the Great), a previous ruler of the Seleucid empire of 'Syria', described as 'king of the north' earlier in the narrative (11:11, *et al.*). The only satisfactory explanation is that a new character has stepped onto Daniel's stage. It seems that the prophet has moved from prototype to antitype, from Antiochus IV Epiphanes to . . . whom? It must be someone yet future, for no one in history fits the picture he paints of this king, or his circumstances. The figure we are looking at is in fact very like the 'beast', 'the man of sin' or 'antichrist', who appears in the New Testament.

Such a conclusion is warranted by the context. The section of narrative in Daniel that indubitably refers to Antiochus IV ends in an indeterminate manner. We read that those who oppose him shall suffer for 'some days'. Then we learn about the falling of the 'wise', 'to refine and to cleanse them and to make them white'; this continues 'until the time of the end'. It is only at this point that the presumptuous king is introduced.

What follows the description of the campaign directed against our presumptuous king by the 'king of the north', and the latter's final overthrow, is even more suggestive,

> At that time shall arise Michael, the great prince who has charge of your people. And there shall be a time of trouble, such as never has been since there was a nation till that time; but at that time your people shall be delivered, every one whose name shall be found written in the book. And many of those who sleep in the dust of the earth shall awake, some to everlasting life, and some to shame and everlasting contempt.

Michael is the archangel, who (we are told here and elsewhere; *cf.* Dan. 10:13,21; Jude 9) has responsibility for Israel. He arises at 'that time' (which, we should recall, is 'the time of the end') because it is supremely 'a time of trouble' for the nation of Israel – recapitulating, though far more intensely, the time of trouble suffered under Antiochus IV.

The period of unprecedented suffering under the presumptuous king is referred to by other prophets. Jeremiah, when speaking about the final restoration of Israel and Judah, says, 'Alas! for that day is great: so that none is like it; it is even the time of Jacob's trouble; but he shall be saved out of it.' (30:7, RV). And we have already seen that Jesus referred to a time of 'great tribulation, such as has not been from the beginning of the world until now' (Mt 24:21). He is speaking in a Jewish context, for this tribulation follows immediately after the Jewish faithful have seen the 'desolating sacrilege spoken of by the prophet Daniel, standing in the holy place' (Mt 24:15).

The reference to Daniel's prediction of a 'desolating sacrilege' is one we have not properly examined. There is, of course, the 'abomination that makes desolate' set up by Antiochus IV in the Temple; but Jesus was obviously not referring to that past event. Among the prophecies of Daniel, however, there is the description of a similar incident. It comes in the context of a passage in which Daniel tells us how 'Gabriel' enlightened him about the future (9:24-27).

The passage begins, 'Seventy weeks of years are decreed concerning your people and your holy city, to finish the transgression, to put an end to sin, and to atone for iniquity, to bring in everlasting righteousness, to seal both vision and prophet, and to anoint a most holy place.' Then we are told that from 'the going forth of the word to restore and build Jerusalem', a period of 69 'weeks of years' (483 lunisolar years of 360 days, the annual unit then in use, or just over 476 actual years) would elapse before 'an anointed one shall be cut off'. This 'word to restore and build Jerusalem' should be identified with the command of the Persian king Artaxerxes I given to Nehemiah, probably in 445 B.C. (Neh. 2:1-9). Dates assigned to events in the ancient world are not always certain, but 476 years after this dating of Ataxerxes' permission to Nehemiah to rebuild Jerusalem brings us exactly into the period (A.D. 30-33) during which, as all agree, Jesus must have been crucified – the 'anointed one [Messiah] . . . cut off'.

Next in this passage from Daniel there follows a prediction of the destruction of Jerusalem, 'The people of the prince who is to come shall destroy the city and the sanctuary.' The prediction was fulfilled when the Romans – the 'people of the prince who is to come' – besieged and devastated the city in A.D. 70. Daniel's prophecy then indicates an indeterminate period following the city's destruction, 'Its [the city's] end shall come with a flood, and to the end there shall be war; desolations are decreed.' (The mention of 'war' and 'desolations' is somewhat reminiscent of Jesus' words about 'wars and rumours of wars'; Mt 24:6.) Finally we come to this statement,

> He shall make a strong covenant with many for one week; and
> for half of the week he shall cause sacrifice and offering to cease;
> and upon the wing of abominations shall come one who makes
> desolate, until the decreed end is poured out on the desolator.

We have reached the future 'desolating sacrilege', one that 'he', presumably the 'prince who is to come', perpetrates at the time of the end. He does this after making 'a strong covenant with many for one week' (seven lunisolar years). This 'prince who is to come' would appear to be the presumptuous king we have been looking at (Daniel 11:36*ff*); he may also be identified with the 'one who makes desolate', though the latter could be a further desecrator, in service of this 'prince'. Whichever way it is, the 'prince' makes a covenant 'with many'. In the context, the 'many' must be those who make 'sacrifice and offering', that is, sons of Israel. In this connection, it is interesting to note that Isaiah, speaking of the end time (28:5,6; *cf.* 24:21-23 *and* 25:6-9), refers to his people making a 'covenant with death' which will not help them 'when the overwhelming scourge passes through' (28:18).

Treachery, tribulation and triumph

Putting all this together, we have the picture of an end time in which the sons of Israel, or 'Jacob', are under pressure to make an agreement with a ruthless world leader. The 'many' succumb and the agreement is made.

Half way through the seven-year period of the agreement, however, the leader betrays those who have trusted him, causing the 'sacrifice and oblation to cease' (an action that presupposes the existence of a Jewish Temple), and perpetrating other abominations – obviously the 'desolating sacrilege' to which Jesus referred. At this point (as Jesus said, Mt 24:16-20), heroics are out of place and flight is the only option. A time of great tribulation follows for the faithful in Israel, who suffer grievous persecution. Nevertheless, as far as the God-fearing in Israel are concerned (the ultimate 'faithful remnant') there are some encouraging promises. There are the words of Jesus, 'For the sake of the elect those days will be shortened' (Mt 24: 22); and there is a prophecy of Jeremiah that they will be 'saved out of' their day of special trouble (Jer. 30:7).

Let us now turn to the book of Revelation, which sheds more light on the 'desolating sacrilege', and the events related to it.

As we saw at the end of Chapter III, in John's book of Revelation there is a 'beast' that corresponds to Daniel's fourth 'beast', which had ten horns. In John's words (13:1),

I saw a beast rising out of the sea, with ten horns and seven heads, with ten diadems upon its horns and a blasphemous name upon its heads.

The 'beast' in each case emerges from the restless sea of nations (Rev. 17:5).

As we have already concluded, both beasts refer to the Roman empire. This identification is corroborated by various features of John's vision, best described in his own words (17:1-6). An angel says to him,

'Come and I will show you the judgement of the great harlot who is seated upon many waters, with whom the kings of the earth have committed fornication, and with the wine of whose fornication the dwellers on earth have become drunk.' And he carried me away in the Spirit into a wilderness, and I saw a woman sitting on a scarlet beast which was full of blasphemous names, and it had seven heads and ten horns. The woman was arrayed in purple and scarlet, and bedecked with gold and jewels and pearls, holding in her hand a golden cup full of abominations and the impurities of her fornication; and on her forehead was written a name of mystery: 'Babylon the great, mother of harlots and of earth's abominations.' And I saw the woman, drunk with the blood of the saints and of the martyrs of Jesus.'

Then the angel explains the mystery of both the beast and the woman (17:8-13),

The beast that you saw was, and is not, and is to ascend from the bottomless pit and go to perdition; and the dwellers upon earth whose names have not been written in the book of life from the foundation of the world, will marvel to behold the beast, because it was, and is not, and is to come. This calls for a mind with wisdom: the seven heads are seven hills on which the woman is seated; they are also seven kings, five of whom are fallen, one is, the other has not yet come, and when he comes he must remain only a little while. As for the beast that was and is not, it is an eighth but it belongs to the seven, and it goes to perdition. And the ten horns that you saw are ten kings who have not yet received royal power, but they are to receive authority as kings for one hour, together with the beast. These are of one mind and give over their power and authority to the beast; they will make war on the Lamb, and the Lamb will conquer them, for he is Lord of lords and Kings of kings, and those with him are called and chosen and faithful.

Corroboration of our identification of the beasts with the Roman empire is supplied, firstly, by the words 'it was, is not, and is to come', suggesting a dramatic 'death and resurrection' of the 'beast' – reflecting the fear, current in John's day, that the evil Nero (who committed suicide in A.D. 68) was miraculously going to reappear; secondly, by some later words, 'The woman that you saw is the great city which has dominion over the kings of the earth.' (17:18). This city, for John, can only have meant Rome. The matter is settled, however, by the fact that the beast's seven heads, as well as being seven kings, are 'seven hills on which the woman is seated'. Ancient tradition has it that Rome was founded, in 753 B.C., on seven hills – the bluffs formed where the Latin plain falls away into the Tiber bed.

John is also told (17:16,17),

The ten horns that you saw, they and the beast will hate the harlot; they will make her desolate and naked, and devour her flesh and burn her up with fire, for God has put it into their hearts to carry out his purpose by being of one mind and giving over their royal power to the beast, until the words of God shall be fulfilled.

It is therefore the beast and the ten kings who are the power behind the empire, essentially 'Roman', though perhaps becoming worldwide in the end through the 'ten kings'.

The harlot, as we have seen, is the city of Rome. In the vision of the fall of this city we are told that 'the merchants of the earth have grown rich with the wealth of her wantonness'. (18:3). She thus represents money, materialism and debauchery. Yet the fact that the Roman power eventually turns on this 'harlot', and the nature of some of the language used of her ('a golden cup full of abominations . . . drunk with the blood of the saints'), plus the fact that as 'Babylon the great' she is described as a 'mystery', may indicate that she also represents a last, corrupt form of religion. It is worth recalling that Julius Caesar transferred the priests of Chaldean Babylon and all their ritual to Rome, thus enhancing his office as *Pontifex Maximus*, or Chief Pontiff, of the pagan religion of Rome. In this manner Rome became 'mystery Babylon'.

The interpretation of the seven heads being seven kings ('five of whom have fallen, one is, the other has not yet come') would appear to refer to five Roman emperors who had already reigned and fallen, the sixth being in power in John's time, while the seventh was yet to come. As these heads have 'a blasphemous name' written upon them (13:1), indicating that they were worshipped as gods, and had 'fallen', which might indicate their violent deaths, the five have been identified with Julius Caesar, Tiberius, Caligula, Claudius and Nero. All these were worshipped as gods, and all came to violent ends. The emperor reigning when John was writing has usually been thought to be Domitian (A.D. 81-96), who assumed divine titles and was assassinated. However, if J.A.T. Robinson (*Redating the New Testament*) is right in placing the composition of Revelation in late A.D. 68, some six months after the suicide of Nero, it would have been Galba, who ruled until January 69. He was followed by Otho, who lasted only three months.

That the seven heads of the beast should be both seven hills and seven kings is in line with common scriptural usage. Daniel, interpreting the vision of the four beasts, initially calls the beast 'four kings' (7:17), yet later describes the fourth beast as 'a fourth kingdom upon earth' (7:23). So two objects, king and kingdom, are represented by the same symbol. 'As for the beast that was and is not', John is told, 'it is an eighth but it belongs to the seven, and it goes to perdition.' In other words, this is the last 'emperor' to arise from within and rule over the 'world' of ancient Rome and apparently beyond, doing so finally through a tenfold confederation. He must be the eleventh horn in Daniel's vision, 'a little one, before which three of the first horns [the ten] were plucked up by the roots' (7:8). So three of the ten 'kings' who have leant support to the emperor, the 'beast', are ultimately to be overthrown by him.

When we meet the 'beast' in Revelation 13, it signifies both empire and emperor – a single symbol denoting both kingdom and king, again following Daniel's usage. The last emperor receives his power from 'the dragon' (13:2), which is Satan (20:2). This emperor (as the 'beast') has a 'mortal wound', but the 'mortal wound was healed' (13:3), or, as we read a little later, he was 'wounded by the sword and yet lived' (13:14) – another reference to some 'miraculous' deliverance from violent death. We may again see an allusion to popular talk about Nero's reappearance, or 'resurrection', John no doubt considering that most bestial of emperors to be one more prototype of the yet future 'beast'. (We might recall that there were constant rumours of Hitler's reappearance following his suicide.)

Nero (like others before him) was to John in one sense more than a prototype. He was a preliminary manifestation, or partial incarnation, of the ultimate author of evil, Satan, who would one day be wholly incarnate in the last 'beast'. This is probably what John meant by 'was, and is not, and is to come': the satanic beast 'was' in Nero, it 'is not' at the time of John, it 'is to come' in a final, exquisitely terrible form. Retrospectively we today can almost find in John's words a secondary future reference – to the 'death' of the Western Roman Empire in A.D. 476, followed by a 'resurrection' in our own day (after earlier attempts at revival, like that of Charlemagne).

Returning to the text of Revelation, we see that the beast's healed 'mortal wound' amazes people. It (or he) is 'allowed to exercise authority for forty-two months' (three and a half years), spending its time uttering 'blasphemies against God', making 'war on the saints' and soliciting worship (13:5-8). In the healed 'mortal wound', as well as in the claim to divinity, we may well discern a demonic recapitulation of Christ's person and work.

The beast has an accomplice, 'another beast' with 'two horns like a lamb', who speaks 'like a dragon' (13:11). He is to be identified with 'the false prophet', who appears later in the vision (16:13; 19:20). Perhaps he is 'the one who makes desolate' of Daniel 9:27. He appears to be a quasi-religious leader, his two lamb-like horns probably indicating the union of religious and political authority in himself. He is, in other words, both prophet and prime minister.

This second beast 'exercises all the authority of the first beast', 'makes the earth and its inhabitants worship the first beast', works great signs, causes an image of the first beast to be set up (slaying those who refuse to worship it), and finally 'causes all, both small and great, both rich and poor, both free and slave, to be marked on the right hand or the forehead, so that no one can buy or sell unless he has the mark, that is, the name of the beast or the number of its name.' (13:11-17). That number, we have already seen, is 666; John calls it 'a human number' (13:18). A worldwide economic protectionist system seems to be envisaged.

The 'number of the beast' has caused endless speculation, with attempts made in particular to link it to the emperor Nero. Yet its significance should be clear to those who know their Bible. The first clue comes from I Kings 10:14, where we read that 'the weight of gold that came to Solomon in one year was six hundred and sixty-six talents of gold'. This numerical correspondence is unlikely to be fortuitous. John knew his Old Testament, and so would most of his intended readers. Here, as elsewhere, he makes an important point in cryptic fashion; he wants it to be obscure to the casual reader, but meaningful to Christians – undergoing fierce persecution by the authorities at the very time he was writing. He gives the Christian reader a further clue, however, by explaining that 666 is 'a human number'.

What does this add up to?

Both clues point in the same direction. In the Bible the number seven stands for completeness, or (divine) perfection. We read in Genesis that God created the world in six 'days', then rested on the seventh; there are thus seven days in the week. In the book of Revelation the number seven is a kind of refrain: seven stars, seven lampstands, seven churches, seven torches 'which are the seven spirits of God', seven seals, and so on. What, then, of six? Quite simply, six is incompleteness, imperfection, a falling short of divine fulness. It is the week without the sabbath, God's day; it is toil without rest; it is work without worship. It is also the fruits of man's labour – 'mammon', money, *gold* (the ultimate symbol of earthly wealth and glory) – whenever these are unconsecrated to God. It is, pre-eminently, man without God, or godlessness. So if 6 (on its own) stands for godlessness, 666 is none other than an unholy trinity. And so we find it in John's book of Revelation: the diabolical trinity of Satan, beast and false prophet.

But we have now come full circle to the 'desolating sacrilege', an event which is also described by St Paul. He writes (II Thess. 2:3-4),

Let no one deceive you in any way; for that day [the day of the Lord] will not come, unless the rebellion comes first, and the man of lawlessness [or 'sin'; RSV *mgn,* and RV] is revealed, the son of perdition, who opposes and exalts himself against every so-called god or object of worship, so that he takes his seat in the temple of God, proclaiming himself to be God.

The supreme act of sacrilege must be this personal appearance of the last emperor in a new Jewish Temple, proclaiming himself God, followed by the erection of his image in 'the holy place' (Mt 24:15), the inner sanctuary or holy of holies of that Temple.

This gross blasphemy marks the breaking by the emperor – 'the beast', 'antichrist', or 'man of sin' – of his seven-year agreement with the Jewish people. Fierce persecution will follow immediately, first directed against those Jews who repudiate allegiance to the emperor and his 'false prophet'. Many, perhaps, will already have been converted to Jesus, their coming Messiah, through the testimony of the 'two witnesses' who are sent from God to the nation, prophesying for three and a half years (Rev. 11:1-13; *cf.* Zech. 4:3,11-14). But the breaking of the covenant with the people as a whole indicates that an effort will be made to crush the entire nation – though the unprecedented tribulation will not be confined to Jews alone. Scripture indicates that this period will see worldwide famine, disease, and fearful natural disasters (Lk 21:25,26; Rev. 6:5-17; 8; 9: 11:13; 16).

The faithful remnant of Israel will nevertheless be saved from this 'time of trouble', as we have seen. John has more to say (7:2-4) on the subject,

> Then I saw another angel ascend from the rising of the sun, with the seal of the living God, and he called with a loud voice to the four angels who had been given power to harm earth and sea, saying, 'Do not harm the earth or the sea or the trees, till we have sealed the servants of our God upon their foreheads.' And I heard the number of the sealed, a hundred and forty-four thousand sealed, out of every tribe of the sons of Israel. . . .

A little later (12:1-6), Israel is symbolised by 'a woman clothed with the sun, with the moon under her feet, and on her head a crown of twelve stars'. A dragon tries to devour her, but she flees into the wilderness, 'where she has a place prepared by God, in which to be nourished for one thousand two hundred and sixty days' (three and a half lunisolar years). She is thus saved from this time of distress. Jeremiah, speaking of 'all the families of Israel' in the 'latter days', records a similar promise, 'Thus says the Lord, "The people who survived the sword found grace in the wilderness; when Israel sought for rest, the Lord appeared to him from afar."' (31:1,2).

We have seen how, at the time of the end, Daniel's presumptuous king, the last 'Roman' emperor, will first be attacked by the 'king of the south' (Egypt), and then 'the king of the north shall rush upon him like a whirlwind' (Dan. 11:40). The target, the context demands, will be the emperor's Palestinian possession, or vassal territory. The 'king of the north' is, according to biblical/historical precedent, likely to be the ruler or rulers of an empire or confederacy that includes what are now Syria, Iraq, the eastern region of Turkey, and Iran; this 'king', we learn, 'shall

come into the glorious land [Palestine] . . . tens of thousands shall fall
. . . the land of Egypt shall not escape . . . the Libyans and Ethiopians
shall follow in his train' (11:41-43). The latter two, lending military
support to 'the king of the north', should be identified with modern Libya,
and northern Sudan (which geographically corresponds to the heartlands
of ancient Ethiopia).

Despite the king of the north's initial successes, 'tidings from the east
and the north shall alarm him', and he plants himself and his forces
'between the sea and the glorious holy mountain', before being himself
overthrown (11:44,45). The 'tidings from the east' may indicate military
movements of the great nations of the east – India, China, Japan, and
others. John sees the waters of the 'great river Euphrates . . . dried up, to
prepare the way for the kings of the east' to assemble themselves 'for
battle on the great day of God the Almighty' (Rev. 16:12,14). Perhaps
Turkey, acting in collusion with or on the orders of the emperor will have
acted to stop the Euphrates waters from reaching Syria and Iraq, that is,
from reaching the territory of 'the king of the north'. (Isaiah, incidentally,
predicts of 'that day' [19:5,16], 'The waters of the Nile will be dried up'
– conceivably a reference to pre-emptive action by Sudan ['Ethiopia']
against Egypt through blocking or diverting the waters of that great river.)
'Tidings . . . from the north' suggests either the mobilisation of the
emperor's European forces, or a move by the Russians.

We have reached Armageddon, when – according to both Old Testament
and New Testament prophecy – God himself arises, together with his
archangel Michael and the hosts of heaven, to take issue with evil.

We have already referred to the return of Jesus in glory to smite 'the
beast and the kings of the earth with their armies gathered to make war
against him' (Rev. 19:11-21). It appears that Jerusalem will be under
siege as the climax approaches. The prophet Zechariah puts it thus (14:2-
5; cf. Zech. 12; Rev. 16:18),

> I will gather all nations against Jerusalem to battle. . . . Then the
> Lord will go forth and fight against those nations. . . . On that
> day his feet shall stand on the Mount of Olives which lies before
> Jerusalem on the east; and the Mount of Olives shall be split in
> two from east to west by a very wide valley . . . and you [faithful
> Jews] shall flee as you fled from the earthquake in the days of
> Uzziah king of Judah. Then the Lord your God will come, and all
> the holy ones with him.

It is at this time, Zechariah indicates, that the Jews will turn nationally to
Jesus as their Messiah, 'him whom they have pierced' (12:10).

We have also looked at the aftermath of all this – a golden age of
universal peace and justice, in which nature is renewed.

There is little more to add beyond emphasising that this climax of history will be the moment of separating true from false, good from evil. Jesus illustrated this in certain stories (Mt 25), as also in these words (Mt 24:36:41),

> Of that day and hour no one knows, not even the angels of heaven, nor the Son, but the Father only. As were the days of Noah, so will be the coming of the Son of man. For as in those days before the flood they were eating and drinking, marrying and giving in marriage, until the day when Noah entered the ark, and they did not know until the flood came and swept them all away, so will be the coming of the Son of man. Then two men will be in the field; one is taken and one is left. Two women will be grinding at the mill; one is taken and one is left.

As the context shows, those who are 'taken' in that day are taken away to judgement; those who are 'left' are left to enter the new and glorious earthly kingdom.

Jesus' return will also see the final gathering of the 'elect', as he calls the last, faithful remnant of Israel. Echoing Isaiah and Jeremiah, Jesus says (Mt 24:30,31),

> Then will appear the sign of the Son of man in heaven, and then all the tribes of the earth will mourn, and they will see the Son of man coming on the clouds of heaven with power and great glory; and he will send his angels with a loud trumpet call, and they will gather his elect from the four winds, from one end of heaven to the other.

VI: Lift-off!

Love and transfiguration

What happens to Christians at the time of the end? What, in particular, should we make of the promise given in the New Testament of a resurrection body to be bestowed on them Jesus returns?

Before answering these questions, let us consider what a Christian is and what is the nature of the new community to which he or she belongs.

In Chapter IV we referred to a question put to Jesus, after his resurrection, by the apostles, 'Lord, will you at this time restore the kingdom to Israel?' (Acts 1:6). We saw how his answer to their question was, in effect, to mind their own business; the restoration of the kingdom to Israel would happen when God saw fit, and there was no reason why they should know when.

That was not all Jesus said, however. He followed up his mild rebuke with the words, 'But you shall receive power when the Holy Spirit has come upon you; and you shall be my witnesses in Jerusalem and in all Judea and Samaria and to the end of the earth.' (Acts 1:8). In his gospel, Luke records similar words spoken by Jesus to the apostles and some others on the evening of the day of his resurrection. Luke describes how the disciples were fearful – and disbelieving – when Jesus suddenly 'stood among them' (24:36). Jesus calmed their fears, then said (24:44-49).

> These are my words which I spoke to you, while I was still with you, that everything written about me in the law of Moses and the prophets and the psalms must be fulfilled. . . . Thus it is written, that the Christ [Messiah] should suffer and on the third day rise from the dead, and that repentance and forgiveness of sins should be preached in his name to all nations, beginning from Jerusalem. You are witnesses of these things. And behold, I send the promise of my Father upon you; but stay in the city, until you are clothed with power from on high.

The 'promise of my Father' refers to something that was to be the seal of their membership of a kingdom quite different from the political, national 'kingdom of Israel' which occupied their thoughts. The kingdom they were entering was 'not of this world', as Jesus had put it to Pontius Pilate (Jn 18:36); it was a spiritual, heavenly kingdom. Or, as Jesus had once explained to the Pharisees when they asked him when the kingdom of God was coming, 'the kingdom of God is within you.' (Lk 17:20,21, RV).

The fulfilment of the 'promise', when the disciples were to be 'clothed with power from on high', occurred at the Jewish Feast of Pentecost, some days after Jesus' final charge to the disciples. A remarkable event took place on that day, according to Luke (Acts 2:1-4). Christians have always believed it to have been the entering of Jesus' own spirit – the 'Holy Spirit' – into the hearts and minds and spirits of his first followers. Jesus had already given a promise to his disciples of the coming, after his death, of 'another Counsellor, to be with you forever, even the Spirit of truth' (Jn 14:15). This Spirit, Jesus explained, was to be that of himself and his Father, for he followed up the promise with these words (Jn 14:18,20,23),

> I will not leave you desolate; I will come to you. . . . In that day you will know that I am in my Father, and you in me, and I in you. . . . If a man loves me, he will keep my word, and my Father will love him, and we will come to him and make our home with him.

However exactly we view the experience of the disciples on that Feast of Pentecost, it transfigured them. They began preaching the bodily resurrection of Jesus from the dead, together with his divinity and, of course, messiahship. Many others believed, and were baptised, and from then on there was a steady increase in the membership of this new community, this spiritual kingdom. So the Church had her birth, a supernatural birth; an outpost of 'the kingdom of heaven' had been established on earth.

What had qualified those first followers of Jesus for membership of this kingdom, for an indwelling of the divine Spirit? The fact that they were Jews? The fact that they had known Jesus in the flesh, or seen him after his resurrection? The fact that they had passed some test, intellectual or moral? No. The Spirit entered them because they loved Jesus.

You cannot manufacture love; it is an instinctive, spontaneous response to beauty. The moral beauty of Jesus – his integrity, his self-giving, *his* love, unstintingly proffered to the unlovely – elicited just such a response from his first followers, as indeed it continues to do from men and women of all ages, climes, and races. Love, the answer of the heart, of the desires, is ultimately the single condition for entry into the spiritual community which is the Church of Jesus Christ, his present kingdom on earth. It is what people *want* that really matters, not what they have done, or can by nature or training make themselves do. For in any case, as Jesus once pointed out to his followers, 'apart from me you can do nothing' (Jn 15:5; *cf.* I Jn 4:19).

Love entails repentance from sin, of course. There can be no meaningful relationship between two people where a recognised wrong is allowed by the guilty party to go unconfessed and thus unforgiven. This is as true between God and man as it is between man and his brother. Love of God also entails trust, or 'faith', in what he commands – that is, active obedience – though this will never, here on earth, be perfect. As we have just seen, Jesus told his followers, 'If a man loves me, he will keep my word.' It is the love that is prior, however, as Jesus makes clear; and where love is present, obedience is bound to follow. 'Lord, you know everything; you know that I love you,' Peter once responded to Jesus – and was given a command to obey (Jn 21:17). The first command for new believers, which Peter was not, is to go through the waters of baptism, signifying a cleansing from or 'dying to' past sin and a rising to new life in Christ (Mt 28:19; Acts 2:38;10:47,48; Rom 6:1-4).

Having thus formally joined the Christian community, the believer's single task in this world *as a Christian* is to reveal Jesus – in his beauty. It is, in other words, to 'witness' to him, in word and deed. The Christian must, in fact, somehow 'live' Jesus before the world. In so doing he or she will call forth from this or that person – who may seem quite hardened or criminal – the same spontaneous love. And so there will be one more penitent, one more human being eager to turn from evil and do good – *Jesus*-good, not the pale *worldly*-good that so often turns out to be evil after all. And the world will be a better place by the presence in its midst of one more forgiven, enlightened, strengthened, forgiving individual.

And it will be a better place by so much more than we think. For the effect for good of only a single Jesus-renewed person within a community is incalculable – as there are countless examples. Christians are the home of the Spirit of God, the Spirit of Jesus, who is (we shall see later) the 'restrainer' of evil and lawlessness (II Thess. 2:7); thus Jesus tells his followers they are 'the salt of the earth' and 'the light of the world' (Mt 5:13a,14a).

Nothing is further from the truth than the idea that Christians can opt out of worldly responsibilities. On the contrary, in being renewed by the Spirit of Jesus, men and women become more perfectly human – more like Jesus himself, the perfect Man. As such they can attend to their human duties all the more effectively. They will certainly, as Christians, enjoy a 'heavenly citizenship', making them in the deepest sense 'strangers and exiles' on earth (Heb. 11:13); yet while they remain in their mortal bodies they will retain all the responsibilities, as well as privileges (let us forget 'rights'!), of their earthly citizenship.

Which means, among other things, working (or not eating), paying tribute to whoever it is due, and honouring and serving the secular authorities in all things lawful (II Thess. 3:10-12; Rom. 13:1-7; I Pet. 2:13-17). It also means co-operating with all men of goodwill, and sometimes taking the lead, in seeking to renew the structures of society where they are inhumane or inadequate. In so doing the Christian will have to accept the moral limitations of those who have not been 'renewed' by the Spirit of Jesus, as also to remember that anything positive achieved will not be permanent. But the aim will be to create, as far as possible, a peaceful and prosperous society, in which the physical, mental and spiritual welfare of all men is adequately cared for.

However close the promised end may be, there is not, and has never been, any justification for sitting and doing nothing while waiting for it to arrive. On the other hand, for Christians to look with eager anticipation for the return of their Lord to take them home is both natural and good. Such an attitude stimulates worthwhile activity. It reminds the Christian worker that men have a potentially eternal destiny, so that nothing done on earth is ever lost; it holds out the promise of rest in moments of weariness; it keeps before the believer the fact that he or she is ultimately accountable to God for service in this life.

It is worthy of recall that a major inspiration for Lord Shaftesbury, the Englishman who in the last century probably did more than any other to improve living conditions for the poor (a grateful nation commemorating the fact in the statue to Eros, or 'love', in London's Piccadilly Circus), was the thought of Jesus' return. Shaftesbury was, as his diaries witness, a man who suffered from frequent depression; it was, in part at least, the 'hope of glory' that made the difference. The light of heaven beyond the darkness of this world kept him going in moments of despair.

What, then, is the Christian 'hope of glory'?

The phrase itself comes in the letter Paul wrote to the Christians at Colossae. In this letter, Paul speaks of 'the mystery hidden for ages and generations but now made manifest to his saints . . . Christ in you, the hope of glory' (Col. 1:26,27b). Once again, we find reiterated the truth that Christians are those in whom Jesus spiritually indwells. This relationship with their divine Lord is, indeed, that alone which constitutes the Christian community a kingdom on earth. Paul uses the word 'kingdom' earlier in the letter, 'He [the Father] has delivered us from the dominion of darkness and translated us to the kingdom of his beloved Son, in whom we have redemption, the forgiveness of sins.' (1:13,14). Jesus is *in* Christians, so they are *in* his kingdom; more, they are *in him* – who has won their 'redemption', the 'forgiveness of sins'. All this, and more, is implied by the phrase 'Christ in you, the hope of glory'.

The 'glory', Paul emphasises, is something Christians already share (for the Father *'has'* delivered/translated us). Believers are in fact gradually being transformed into the image of their Lord, as he tells those at Corinth (II Cor. 3:16-18),

> When a man turns to the Lord the veil is removed. Now the Lord
> is the Spirit, and where the Spirit of the Lord is, there is freedom.
> And we all, with unveiled face, beholding the glory of the Lord,
> are being changed [or 'transfigured'] into his likeness from one
> degree of glory to another; for this comes from the Lord, who is
> the Spirit.

Yet Paul tells Christians above all to look forward. Their special relationship with Jesus and thus with their Father-God – this 'Christ in you, the hope of glory' – may be something they enjoy now, but it also points to something future. Later in the letter to the Colossians Paul explains what this paradoxical earthly/heavenly, present/future axis means for everyday living (Col. 3:1-4),

> If you then have been raised with Christ, seek the things that are
> above, where Christ is, seated at the right hand of God. Set your
> minds on things that are above, not on things that are on the earth.
> For you have died, and your life is hid with Christ in God. When
> Christ who is our life appears, then you also will appear with him
> in glory.

'Glory' keeps breaking through in Paul's letters; it is as if he cannot help thinking about it. In this last passage it is linked to Jesus' coming again, his appearing. We must now examine the latter in relation to the Christian's 'hope of glory'.

Kept from the hour

One of the promises given to believers in the New Testament is that they will be delivered from God's future wrath. For instance, Paul promises the Roman Christians that 'since . . . we are now justified by his [Christ's] blood, much more shall we be saved by him from the wrath of God' (Rom. 5:9). In his first letter to the Christians at Thessalonica, Paul speaks glowingly of how they 'turned to God from idols, to serve a living and true God, and to wait for his Son from heaven, whom he raised from the dead, Jesus who delivers us from the wrath to come' (I Thess. 1:9,10). In the same letter he declares, speaking in the context of the return of Jesus to take his people to be with him in heaven, 'For God has not destined us for wrath, but to obtain salvation through our Lord Jesus Christ.' (5:9). So he exhorts them, 'Therefore encourage one another and build one another up, just as you are doing.' (5:11).

This promise is important as we consider the Christian's status in relation to the last 'time of trouble', the unprecedented tribulation. In his book of Revelation, John makes it clear that 'the great tribulation' (Rev. 7:14) represents (among other things) a pouring out of God's wrath upon a godless world. He tells us how, in that fearful time, men will call 'to the mountains and rocks, "Fall on us and hide us from the face of him who is seated on the throne, and from the wrath of the Lamb; for the great day of their wrath has come, and who can stand before it?"' (6:16,17). Or again (15:1; 16:1),

> I saw another portent in heaven, great and wonderful, seven angels with seven plagues, which are the last, for with them the wrath of God is ended. . . . Then I heard a loud voice from the temple telling the seven angels, 'Go and pour out on the earth the seven bowls of the wrath of God.

There are other such statements.

It would seem curious, on the face of it, if Christians – though promised tribulation in this world in a general sense (Jn 16:33b) – were to be required to go through this time of supreme tribulation, this day of God's wrath. Happily, the indications in the New Testament are that they will *not* be so required, as G.B. Stanton has demonstrated (K*ept from the Hour*, Zondervan, 1956).

One such indication is a promise given early in the book of Revelation to 'the angel of the church in Philadelphia' (3:7). The church in question is one of 'the seven churches' to whom John is bidden to send his prophetic book (1:11). But there are grounds for believing that the promise given to that church is valid for the entire Church of Jesus Christ, not merely for a local congregation or assembly in John's day.

As well as all the general prophecies about the last days (many of which we considered in the last chapter), John includes at the beginning of his book seven special messages, or letters, to these seven churches. The messages, he claims, have been given him by Jesus himself (1:12 – 2:1). The seven letters appear to have several applications. It is true that they were, firstly, addressed to seven existing churches – that is, different Christian assemblies – in the western-most province of Asia Minor; very probably every letter went to all seven (*cf*. 2:7,11,17, etc). But the fact that there were seven (a number in scripture denoting completeness, or perfection, as we have seen) suggests that they were also representative, or typical. Similarly, the reference to 'seven golden lampstands', which 'are the seven churches' (1:20), indicates that what is intended is more than particular assemblies. The seven churches seem, in fact, to reflect seven different types of church (and perhaps kinds of individual Christian) that can be found in any location at any period of time. We can go further: when we consider the nature of each church in the order they are given, there emerges something that looks very like a thumbnail sketch of church history.

Be the last point as it may, it is clear that the letter to the church in Philadelphia is of more than local significance. What of that church's character? The message given through John begins, 'I have set before you an open door, which no one is able to shut; I know that you have but little power, and yet you have kept my word and have not denied my name.' (3:8). The Philadelphian congregation is apparently missionary minded, and faithful to its Lord, but of little worldly strength. Like the community in Smyrna, which is promised tribulation for 'ten days' (2:10), it receives no rebuke; and it may be significant that the name of the city in which it foregathers – *philadelphia* – means 'brotherly or sisterly love'. It can therefore appropriately represent the true Church of God, unmixed with hypocritical elements. And so we come to the special promise given to it, and thus (it seems reasonable to conclude) to every believer, 'Because you have kept my word of patient endurance, I will keep you from the hour of trial which is coming on the whole world, to try those who dwell upon the earth.' (3:10).

The 'hour of trial' here promised is evidently not local, for it is 'coming on the whole world'. Indeed, the phrase 'those who dwell upon the earth' suggests that every living person will have to endure this time. It can only be future; the persecutions of the past, though often traumatic, were limited to one group, and usually to one country or area. It most obviously refers to the last 'great tribulation' of which John, echoing Jesus (Mt 24:21), later speaks. So we have a promise given to all true believers that they will not be required to pass through this period of unparalleled world distress, this outpouring of God's wrath.

Some have queried this conclusion, arguing that a better rendering of the Greek in this promise is '*through* the hour', not '*from* the hour'. In other words, Christians will have to suffer the hour of trial with everyone else, though they will be specially sustained or preserved through it. There are, however, no grounds for translating the common Greek word *ek* by anything other than 'out of', or 'from' – the normal meaning in such a context (see *A Greek-English Lexicon*, Liddell and Scott, Oxford University Press). There is certainly no precedent for translating it 'through', in the sense of 'in' or 'during', for which there are other Greek prepositions. But what seems to clinch the matter is the fact that the promise is of being kept not merely from the *trial*, but from the *hour of trial*. That is, the promise holds out exemption from the period of trial, not just from the trial during that period.

So, according to the promise given in this message to 'the angel of the church in Philadelphia', the Church is not going to experience the world's darkest hour. The Jewish 'elect', it is clear, have to go through it, although they will be given special protection; others, too, will survive – though John also tells us that many will be martyred 'for their testimony to Jesus' (Rev. 20:4; *cf.* 6:9-11; 7:9-14; 14:12,13). The latter will probably have become followers of Jesus through reading the scriptures (the book of Revelation, especially) during the tribulation period; indeed, in John's vision there appears, among all the plagues and woes, an 'angel flying in midheaven, with an eternal gospel to proclaim to those who dwell on earth, to every nation and tribe and tongue and people' (Rev. 14:6,7). God will not be without witness during this grim time – which is as we would expect. But to return to our original point: Christian believers alive on earth as the hour of trial approaches are destined to escape that hour altogether.

There is a passage in Paul's second letter to the Christians at Thessalonica that bears on this matter (part of it was quoted in the last chapter). The Thessalonians thought that the 'day of the Lord' was upon them. Paul (II Thess. 2:1-8) reassures them it was not,

> Now concerning the coming of our Lord Jesus Christ and our assembling to meet him, we beg you, brethren, not to be quickly shaken in mind or excited, either by spirit or by word, or by letter purporting to come from us, to the effect that the day of the Lord has come. Let no one deceive you in any way; for that day will not come, unless the rebellion comes first, and the man of lawlessness [or 'sin'] is revealed, the son of perdition, who opposes and exalts himself against every so-called god or object of worship, so that he takes his seat in the temple of God, proclaiming himself to be God. Do you not remember that when I was still with you I told you this? And you know what is restraining him now so that he may be revealed in his time. For the mystery of lawlessness is already at work; only he who now restrains it will do so until he is out of the way. And then the lawless one will be revealed, and the Lord Jesus will slay him with the breath of his mouth and destroy him by his appearing and his coming.

Paul is telling them that the 'day of the Lord' (the whole last period of God's wrath leading up to Jesus' coming in glory) will not occur until 'the man of sin' (John's 'antichrist', or 'beast') is revealed. We have already seen how this monstrously evil being will commit the supreme sacrilege of proclaiming himself divine in the very Temple of God, where also his image will be set up, and how fearful persecution of faithful Jews (and others) will follow. Let us look again at what Paul says after describing the man of sin,

> You know what is restraining him [the man of sin] now so that he may be revealed in his time. For the mystery of lawlessness is

already at work; only he who restrains it will do so until he is out
of the way. And then the lawless one will be revealed. . . .

There is in the world a restraining person or influence that holds evil
in check; until this 'restrainer' is taken out of the way, 'the man of sin' or
'lawless one' cannot make his appearance. Attempts have been made to
identify the 'restrainer' as the Roman Empire, or Human Government in
the abstract, or the Jewish State, or even an individual, like the apostle
James. But none of these suggestions is remotely satisfactory.

As we all know, there is only one person or influence restraining evil
and lawlessness in the world in a general sense – the Spirit of God. The
Spirit it was who sought to control man and restrain his wickedness in
the time of Noah, though God finally decided this was a lost cause,
whereupon he destroyed mankind in the flood – apart from righteous
Noah, saved together with his family in the ark (Gen. 6:1-8). Paul is
saying to the Thessalonians that God's Spirit, now resident on earth in
the Church, has to be 'out of the way', or 'taken out of the way' (RV),
before 'the man of sin' can appear. From which it is clear that the Church
herself must be removed from the earth before he appears. There cannot
be a Church without the indwelling Spirit.

Paul specifically says in introducing this item of teaching that his
concern is 'the coming of our Lord Jesus Christ and our assembling to
meet him'. This 'assembling' does not, of course, refer to an assembling
for worship, but to the gathering up of all Christians to meet Jesus 'in the
air' when he comes to take them to heaven. (We shall look at this more
closely below). So he is not introducing into this passage the thought of
the Church's 'removal' from the earth as something new.

Paul appears to refer to this 'removal' a little later. Having said
something about the Satanic activities of 'the man of sin', and his 'wicked
deception' of the bulk of humanity (II Thess. 2:9-11), he continues, 'But
we are bound to give thanks to God always for you, brethren beloved by
the Lord, because God chose you from the beginning to be saved, through
sanctification by the Spirit and belief in the truth.' (II Thess. 2:13). The
words echo some others in his first letter, already partially quoted, 'For
God has not destined us for wrath, but to obtain salvation through our
Lord Jesus Christ, who died for us so that whether we wake or sleep we
might live with him.' (I Thess. 5:9,10). In these verses, 'saved' or
'salvation' seems to have, as well as a general reference to the Christian's
status, more specific reference to the fact that believers living in the last
time will be kept safe, or away, from the savagery of 'the man of sin',
from the outpouring of God's wrath; in other words, we here have further
(implied) assurance that Christians will be removed from earth before
the last great tribulation begins. This is borne out by the promise that

Christians shall 'live with him', which in the context refers to the fact that believers – those in the last days who are alive (who 'wake'), as well as those who have died (who 'sleep') – are to be taken to live with Jesus in heaven, thus escaping the 'wrath' that falls on a godless world.

Just how will Christians, alive and dead, be taken to live with Jesus in heaven? How, in particular, will those still living on earth be 'removed', or taken away?

'We shall be changed'

When he was giving some final teaching and encouragement to his disciples in the upper room on the night of his betrayal and arrest, Jesus included something about his second coming. 'Let not your hearts be troubled,' he said, 'believe in God, believe also in me. In my Father's house are many rooms; if it were not so, would I have told you that I go to prepare a place for you? And when I go and prepare a place for you, I will come again and will take you to myself, that where I am you may be also.' (Jn 14:1-3).

Jesus was explaining that when he rejoined his Father in heaven ('my Father's house'), which he did after his resurrection, he would make a home there for his followers, in due course returning to take them to it. Some have suggested that this is only a promise of his coming for them at death. But the words 'I will come again', in direct antithesis to the words 'I go', seem to preclude such an interpretation. Nowhere else in the New Testament is death seen as an occasion on which Jesus 'comes' for the believer. It is, rather, the moment when the latter 'falls asleep', leaving behind his body so that he can be 'at home with the Lord' (I Cor. 15:18; I Thess. 4:13; II Cor. 5:8).

So Jesus is one day coming again to take his followers to heaven. It will perhaps be pointed out that he did not 'come again' in the lifetime of those to whom he was speaking, so (some might object) his promise was empty. Such an objection is unreasonable. First we must remember that when Jesus was speaking to his disciples in Palestine he was often looking beyond them to those who would join the Church later. When he talked of himself as 'the good shepherd', for example, he referred to 'other sheep, not of this fold' – a reference to those from among the Gentiles (*i.e.* those other than the Jews, who *were* of 'this fold') who would become believers after his departure (Jn 10:14-16). And some of his parables, like those on the 'kingdom of heaven' (Mt 13), and his teaching on the end of the age and the coming of the Son of man (Mt 24 and 25; Lk 21), seem to envisage later believers – though such prophetic scenarios are not given a definite timescale. In other words, promises Jesus gave in person to his followers are usually intended for future believers as well. So Jesus' promise 'I will come again and will take you to myself' is meant as much for today's believers as it was for those to whom it was first given.

There is, however, a second point to make in answer to our hypothetical objection: the promise to those first disciples is actually going to be fulfilled. For when Jesus comes again to take Christians to himself and to 'my Father's house', he will be coming not only for believers who are alive, but also for those who have died, or 'fallen asleep'. Among the latter will be the first disciples.

In his first letter to the Thessalonians, Paul .(4:13, 15-17) describes this coming in more detail,

> We would not have you ignorant, brethren, concerning those who are asleep, that you may not grieve as others do who have no hope. . . . For this we declare to you by the word of the Lord, that we who are alive, who are left until the coming of the Lord, shall not precede those who have fallen asleep. For the Lord himself will descend from heaven with a cry of command, with the archangel's call, and with the sound of the trumpet of God. And the dead in Christ will rise first; then we who are alive, who are left, shall be caught up together with them in the clouds to meet the Lord in the air; and so shall we always be with the Lord. Therefore comfort one another with these words.

He describes the same event to the Christians at Corinth (I Cor. 15:51,52),

> Lo! I tell you a mystery. We shall not all sleep, but we shall all be changed, in a moment, in the twinkling of an eye, at the last trumpet. For the trumpet will sound, and the dead will be raised imperishable, and we shall be changed.

These descriptions of Jesus' coming to give both dead and living believers new bodies, and to take them to heaven, do not sound much like the coming John describes at the end of his book of Revelation. There, Jesus is seated on a white horse; he is the 'Faithful and True', who 'in righteousness . . . judges and makes war'; his eyes are 'a flame of fire'; he is clad in 'a robe dipped in blood', and 'the armies of heaven, arrayed in fine linen, white and pure', follow him 'on white horses.' Nor, can it be said, do descriptions of Jesus' coming for believers correspond very closely to the sentence already quoted from Paul's letter to the Colossians (3:4), 'When Christ who is our life appears, then you also will appear with him in glory.' There is little correspondence between the two types of description because they refer to different events: Jesus comes for believers *before the commencement* of the 'hour of trial', the period of great tribulation, while he comes to overthrow the enemies of

God and inaugurate his earthly kingdom *at the end* of it – accompanied by his already resurrected Church as well as by angelic hosts.

Is there anything in the book of Revelation, besides the promise given to the church in Philadelphia, indicating that the Church is to be removed from the earth before the terrible events it describes?

It may be significant that the Church is never mentioned by name as existing on earth during the tribulation period, though the more general term 'saints' is used. More suggestive is the possibility that the writers's experience of being spiritually caught up through 'an open door' (Rev. 4:1,2) in order to stand in the courts of heaven (where he apparently remains for the whole of his vision, looking down upon earth) reflects the catching up of the Church described by Paul. John immediately (4:2b-4) describes what confronts him,

> A throne stood in heaven, with one seated on the throne! And he who sat there appeared like jasper and carnelian, and round the throne was a rainbow that looked like an emerald. Round the throne were twenty-four thrones, and seated on the thrones were twenty-four elders, clad in white garments, with golden crowns upon their heads.

The throne is presumably that of Christ, and the elders seem to be representative of the translated or resurrected Church, the 'new song' they sing corroborating this identification (5:9,10, *esp.* AV).

We have established that Jesus' coming again for his believing people will be before the world's 'hour of trial'. If this is the case, there is nothing – no event predicted by the prophets, Jesus, Paul or anyone else – needing to be fulfilled prior to that day. The New Testament as a whole gives just such an impression, that Jesus' coming again for his Church is imminent; it does not have to be soon, yet it could be at any moment. As Jesus himself said, 'Watch therefore, for you know neither the day nor the hour.' (Mt 25:13).

'I will come again and will take you to myself, that where I am you may be also.' This promise, given by Jesus to his disciples in the upper room, is the Christian's perennial hope and comfort.

VII: Watching for the Morning

Shadows and substance

C.S. Lewis – as many will know from the film 'Shadowlands' – was an Oxford don who besides being a scholar, and besides having a sadly curtailed though joyful marriage, wrote seven books about children who keep passing between this world and an entirely different one called 'Narnia'. 'Farewell to Shadowlands'is the final chapter of the seventh volume, *The Last Battle*. At the end of this chapter the children meet Aslan.

> *Aslan turned to them and said:*
>
> *'You do not yet look so happy as I mean you to be.'*
>
> *Lucy said, 'We're so afraid of being sent away, Aslan. And you have sent us back into our own world so often.'*
>
> *'No fear of that,' said Aslan. 'Have you not guessed?'*
>
> *Their hearts leaped and a wild hope rose within them.*
>
> *'There **was** a real railway accident,' said Aslan softly. 'Your father and mother and all of you are – as you used to call it in Shadowlands – dead. The term is over: the holidays have begun. The dream is ended: this is the morning.'*
>
> *And as He spoke He no longer looked to them like a lion; but the things that began to happen after that were so great and so beautiful that I cannot write them. And for us this is the end of all the stories, and we can most truly say that they all lived happily ever after. But for them it was only the beginning of the real story. All their life in this world and all their adventures in Narnia had only been the cover and the title page: now at last they were beginning Chapter One of the Great Story which no one on earth has read: which goes on for ever: in which every chapter is better than the one before.*

Is this really how it will be?

C.S. Lewis believed that in this world we are in 'shadowlands'; real substance is only to be found in heaven. That is also what the New Testament teaches. Paul writes of religious observances in his letter to the Colossians, 'These are only a shadow of what is to come; but the substance belongs to Christ.' (2:17). Or again, writing to the Corinthians (II Cor. 4:16-18),

> We do not lose heart. Though our outer nature is wasting away, our inner nature is being renewed every day. For this slight momentary affliction is preparing for us an eternal weight of glory

beyond all comparison, because we look not to the things that are seen but to the things that are unseen; for the things that are seen are transient, but the things that are unseen are eternal.

How do these truths tie up with the Christian hope as we have defined it in the preceding chapter?

It is important to remember the *two* aspects of life after death for the Christian – the time between his or her death and Jesus' coming again, and the time after that coming again, when he or she will have been 'further clothed' with an immortal body (II Cor. 5:4). Let us consider each aspect.

As we have seen, the New Testament speaks of Christian believers who have died as 'those who are asleep', or 'those who have fallen asleep in Christ' (I Thess. 4:13; I Cor. 15:18). These are Paul's words. Jesus himself spoke of his friend Lazarus, who had died, as one who had 'fallen asleep' (Jn 11:11) – though strictly speaking this preceded the Christian era, which only began when the disciples received the gift of the Holy Spirit at Pentecost. In sleep we are not fully conscious, and time passes quickly, sometimes in a flash. It therefore seems possible that Christians who have died and are 'asleep in Christ' – or, as Paul puts it elsewhere, 'away from the body' and therefore 'at home with the Lord' (II Cor. 5:8) – will hardly be aware of a lapse of time before experiencing the great consummation, the day of resurrection.

Life beyond the grave but prior to the resurrection will be a disembodied existence. Though the faithful dead will have a happy awareness of Jesus' comforting presence, their mode of consciousness may well be analogous to that of sleep. Perhaps, like us, they will dream, though theirs will be good dreams. In any case, they will be resting – at peace. Reverting to the question of the passage of time: there seems every reason to believe that just as we, after a deep sleep, wake to the morning sunshine seemingly only a few moments after we have laid our head on the pillow, so the faithful departed will experience the joy of longed-for morning, the day of resurrection itself when their Lord returns, hard on the heels of their experience of death.

We on earth have consciously to wait for Jesus' coming again, when living believers will be 'changed' rather than resurrected. We long for the 'redemption of our bodies' (Rom. 8:23), and waiting can seem tedious; indeed, death will probably intervene. It seems likely, therefore, that those who have already entered the nearer presence of their Lord through death will be spared an age-long wait.

What, then, of life in the 'resurrection' body? What of life *after* Jesus has come again?

God has pledged, through his apostle Paul, that he will 'change our lowly body to be like his [Jesus'] glorious body' (Phil. 3:21). We are therefore to be like the resurrected Christ. Indeed, we are to be like him in the glorified form he will assume when he returns. As John writes, 'When he appears we shall be like him.' (I Jn 3:2).

Let us turn to Paul again. In his first letter to the Corinthians he likens the earthly body to a seed, while the resurrection body is the fully developed plant, 'What is sown is perishable, what is raised is imperishable. It is sown in dishonour, it is raised in glory. It is sown in weakness, it is raised in power. It is sown a physical body, it is raised a spiritual body.' (15:42b-44). In other words, the resurrection body surpasses the earthly body as – for example – a rosebush in full bloom surpasses a rose hip, or the mighty oak an acorn. This is just one measure of how much more substantial, how much more glorious, how much more powerful resurrection life will be than life here on earth.

We can learn more by looking at the resurrection appearances of Jesus.

After his resurrection Jesus possessed all earthly attributes, plus many more. If this seems paradoxical we should not be surprised, for the truth – as scientists today tirelessly assure us – is frequently paradoxical. The resurrected Jesus had, in his own words, 'flesh and bones'; he could be touched and handled, so that 'doubting Thomas' could feel the wound in his side; he could breathe, walk and talk quite naturally; he could kindle a fire and eat a piece of boiled fish; he could, most significant of all, break bread with his friends – he could and did enjoy warm, vital fellowship. In other words, he was utterly and gloriously human. (See Lk 24:39; Jn 20:27; Jn 20:22 and Lk 24:13-27; Jn 21:9-13 and Lk 24:42,43; Lk 24:30 and Jn 21:9-13.)

On the other hand, Jesus was able in his resurrection body to appear and disappear at will, not only passing through closed doors but through solid rock. For we must understand that the 'great stone', rolled to the door of Jesus' tomb and sealed (with iron, probably) by the Jewish guard, was rolled away – in an earthquake that accompanied the visitation of 'an angel of the Lord' – not to let Jesus out but to allow his disciples in (Mt 27:60,66; 28:2). After his resurrection Jesus in fact inhabited another dimension of existence, appearing (in our dimension) intermittently to his followers over a period of forty days to assure them he was alive, as well as to give them further teaching. Finally, at the end of the forty days, Jesus left his disciples visibly, passing into the heavens when 'a cloud' took him out of their sight (Lk 24:50,51; Acts 1:9). In that heavenly realm he was able to enjoy uninterrupted fellowship with God the Father, and there he still resides, in 'the power of an indestructible life' (Heb. 8:1; 9:24; 7:16b). From there, too, he 'will come in the same manner as you saw him go into heaven' (Acts 1:11b).

Can it really be true that 'we shall be like him'?

This is what we are promised – which means that every one of the attributes of Jesus will one day be enjoyed by Christian believers.

Christians have already been adopted into Jesus' family as 'children of God', so how could it be otherwise? (See Gal. 4:4-7; I Jn 3:1,2).

Of course, the believer's resurrection life will not be in the context of this earth – though Christians *are* promised that one day they 'shall reign on earth' (Rev. 5:10; 20:6; *cf.* II Tim. 2:12; Mt 19:28). Resurrection life will be in the context of heaven.

Yet even heaven will not be for ever. The ultimate goal, towards which all life is moving, is 'a new heaven and a new earth' (Rev. 21:1). One day there will be an entirely new creation, no longer heaven over against earth, but a marriage of heaven and earth, a new, all-inclusive dimension of life where 'the holy city, new Jerusalem' will be the dwelling place of God and man (Rev. 21:2-4).

A parable

Let me conclude with something personal – a kind of parable.

Some forty years ago I was – like every other young, male British subject who was not ill, or who did not have conscientious scruples – called up to do National Service. I became a Royal Air Force policeman and was immediately drafted to Cyprus. Being a policeman, I often had to do the night shift from 11 p.m. to 7 a.m. guarding installations.

Those nights seemed endless, and I would break them up by walking round the perimeter fence, examining vehicles or buildings for anything unusual, or flashing the searchlight beyond the barbed wire. Apart from my own movements, and the very occasional sound of some commotion from the direction of the nearby town, nothing happened on those night duties – except what always happened above me, the movement of the stars.

It was up at the stars I would look for interest and, in a sense, for comfort. Shining so brightly, they seemed to be my friends; they told me how the night was progressing. And especially, those night skies told me of the approach of dawn.

For during the months of my assignment to these duties the planet Venus was in her mode as the morning star, and as the night grew long and wearisome I would watch for her appearance over the eastern horizon. She would climb into the sky, serene and beautiful, outshining every other heavenly body, a sign and a seal to each tired night watcher that the darkness would shortly be dispelled, that day was soon to arrive.

Jesus said, 'I am . . . the bright morning star.' (Rev. 22:16).

Of all the images in scripture given us to describe the nature or role of Jesus, I have found this teasingly cryptic identification of him with the morning star to be the most haunting. It constitutes some of the very last words of the book of Revelation – indeed, of the whole New Testament.

Written by the apostle John, in exile on the Greek island of Patmos, the words were certainly among the last to be written. John passed them on to us as a message from the risen Lord.

All the New Testament images used to describe Jesus – the true bread, the light of the world, the vine, the good shepherd, the Word, the bridegroom – are given to enrich our understanding of him. What special truth is represented by the image of him as the morning star?

It is quiet reflection that helps us understand these things, and I had plenty of time for reflection during those long Cyprus nights on guard duty. And it was at that time, when morning by morning I watched the star as it appeared, then climbed into the sky, finally to be banished by the brilliance of the rising sun, that I realised I was looking at a vast, cosmic visual aid. It was God's commentary on my efforts to comprehend one of the less obvious truths of scripture.

Jesus, I reflected, has told us he is the morning star. But Jesus is also (as I recalled from a much-loved carol) known to Christians as the 'sun of righteousness'. And then I saw the symmetry. Jesus as the morning star is the last image in the New Testament. It is a final truth for Christians to grasp and ponder. The last image in the Old Testament, a last great truth given to the sons of Jacob, is that of the future rising of the sun of righteousness. It occurs – as we have aleady seen – in the last chapter of the last book of the Old Testament, that of the prophet Malachi, almost certainly the last of the prophets before Christ. 'For you who fear my name,' he declares as God's spokesman, 'the sun of righteousness shall rise, with healing in its wings' (4:2).

So we have the two images – sun of righteousness and morning star. The former is especially relevant for the people descended from Jacob/Israel, still harbouring national hopes and aspirations, an image associated with a final day of judgement. For, a few sentences after speaking of the sun of righteousness, Malachi concludes his prophecy with a reference to 'the great and terrible day of the Lord' (4:5). The latter is relevant for Christians, believers in Jesus as Saviour and Lord, an image associated with his coming again. John signs off Revelation (22:20) with the words, 'He who testifies to these things says, "Surely I am coming soon." Amen. Come, Lord Jesus!'

Why, I asked myself, does scripture tell the sons of Israel to look and long for their ultimate fulfilment in one last great dawn, when the power and splendour of the rising sun will scatter the shades of night, the evils of the darkness, whereas the same scripture tells the Christian to look and long for that silent, almost secret rising of the morning star *before* the dawn?

I began to understand.

The fact of Jesus' coming again is held out by the New Testament to Christians as an incentive, an inspiration and, above all, a comfort. We have already cited Paul's words concluding his description of Jesus' coming to take believers home. 'Comfort one another with these words,' he says (I Thess. 4:18). He similarly exhorts the Corinthians, after describing this coming, 'Therefore, my beloved brethren, be steadfast, immovable, always abounding in the work of the Lord, knowing that in the Lord your labour is not in vain.' (I Cor. 15:58). The certainty of Jesus' coming again, to transform and lead to glory the faithful living and dead, is the great constant, an anchor. It is a source of joy and strength when all around is crumbling. And that coming (we have already emphasised) is *imminent*. That is to say, for every Christian, past and present, it could have been, or could yet be, 'today'. 'Watch therefore,' we are told, 'for you know neither the day nor the hour.'

The idea of 'imminence' presents a problem, however, as we have noted. Certain events, notably the appearance of antichrist, are predicted by Jesus (and others) as having to occur before his return in glory; how, then, can a Christian expect Jesus' return at any time? He will surely be looking first for the fulfilment of these predictions. Yet this paradox has been resolved by employing the scientific principle that where there is an apparent contradiction we must look for some new, probably important truth. It was, indeed, in those far off Cyprus days – or rather nights – that I first realised the answer was staring me in the face: Jesus' return for Christians is a coming – like that of the morning star – quietly, unostentatiously *before* the dawn; his return for Israel is the dawn itself, a brilliant and glorious rising of the sun, banishing every evil shadow.

Now I am again in Cyprus, my life having unexpectedly come full circle. I write these words just a few miles from the Air Force camp where I was once stationed, in the town I used regularly to visit and where I now live and work. I still enjoy the night sky, sometimes (in season) pulling back the bedroom curtain to contemplate Venus as she rises a little before dawn. As I look, I ponder how events have unrolled since those long nights when I watched for the same 'morning star' to appear, and it seems to me that at this moment in history the world is journeying into darkness, not light.

People say, to comfort themselves perhaps, that the darkest hour of night comes just before dawn. It may be true, if only subjectively. Yet there are better grounds than this for keeping hope intact.

Two thousand years ago wise men were led by the bright shining of a star to a King, born in a stable. In a benighted world a single point of light brought them hope and joy, because it signified their salvation. I too am looking for a single point of light to pierce the present darkness. I am awaiting the harbinger of a dawn soon to break over the earth, at the return of the King in his glory. I am waiting, and will go on waiting, I am watching, and will go on watching, for 'the bright morning star'.

Index